# The Essential Guide to
# IGCSE: Additional Math
# 2017-2019

Suited for any student
who prepares for IGCSE Additional Math (0606)
from June 2017 to November 2019

Written By

Harim Yoo

Essential Math Series

## Legal Notice

Copyright © 2019 by Harim Yoo
ISBN : 9781089816089
Imprint : Independently published

All rights reserved. This publication or any portion thereof may not be copied, replicated, distributed, or transmitted in a any form or by any means whether electronically or mechanically whatsoever. It is illegal to produce derivative works from this publication, in whole or in part, without the prior written permission of the publisher or author.

# About the Author

The author, Harim Yoo, graduated from Northwestern University (B.A. in Mathematics and Economics) in 2012. Harim also served in the ROK/U.S Army as a KATUSA sergeant in the 2nd infantry division from 2012-2014.

Since his ETS from duty, he found his passion for teaching and educating bright students. He gradually developed his career as a lecturer at Masterprep and has now been recognized as one of the leading lecturers in Apgujeong, Seoul.

Harim is currently dedicating his time to produce mathematical prep-books for junior high/high school students to simplify learning methods to effectively learn the core concepts and problem-solving strategies, writing on the bulky series called **Essential Math Series**, including *The Essential Workbook for SAT Math Level 2*.

# Preface & Acknowledgment

The first year I encountered IGCSE Additional Math as a tutoring subject was 2014. When I tutored students from an international school in Seoul, I was surprised by the coverage of curriculum that reaches to Calculus at 10th grade, although the materials were not advanced enough to be called as a year-long Calculus course. Past few years, I looked for textbooks or prepatory books that could help students learn and master the materials. I found some textbooks commonly referred to as Addmath books, one by Singaporean authors and other by Australian authors. Both books I found were illustrative, but they were quite long to cover within a short period of time.

Nevertheless, as I taught more students, I felt an urge to write a book that could guide students learn the materials quickly and effectively, for an instance, over the summer break. I tried to explain what IGCSE: Additional Math(0606) focuses on by covering examples typically asked for the end-of-year test every year.

This is the first edition of *The Essential Guide to IGCSE Additional Math* for 2017-2019 coursework, so I expect to update with new chapters at the end of this year for 2020-2022 version. Nonetheless, as I already used this to some of my students, I reckon it is good enough to be published for the first edition. If you think you have found an error, please let me know through the email jamesyhr@gmail.com.

The book is designed to cover possibly all materials for IGCSE Additional Math (0606) 2017-2019 courework, a supplement to my online lecture series at Masterprep in South Korea. Some of the questions you will encounter in this book are types of questions that are likely to appear in the end-of-year test. Those who take IB MYP could study with this book to prepare for IB coursework. For students who study Addmath in a two-year course, one should expect to study from Chapter 1 to Chapter 12 in the first year, while other materials are covered in the second year. For students who study Addmath in a one-year course, the first semester covers from Chapter 1 to Chapter 11, and the second semester covers all the other materials. I designed this book to contain the most essential knowledge required for IGCSE Additional Math. Since this book contains less than 200 practice questions, if you want to finish learning and reviewing the materials, you could do it within 50 days.

Special thanks to my family for unconditional support, Mr. Kwon at MasterPrep for unceasing mentorship, and Director Shim as a great role-model and a leader. Finally, I am deeply thankful of God our Lord who led me to this industry ever since 2012 when I graduated from college. I never expected to write any prep-book on high school mathematics while I was in college. Nonetheless, a series of events in life gave me this priceless opportunity to help students on mathematical journeys during their youth. Thus, I sincerely hope this book turns out to be beneficial for all readers who study with it.

Harim Yoo

# Contents

| | |
|---|---:|
| About the Author | 3 |
| Preface & Acknowledgment | 5 |
| **1 Set Theory** | **11** |
|    1.1 Types of Set | 12 |
|    1.2 Perform Basic Set Arithmetic | 13 |
|    1.3 Important Principles | 14 |
| **2 System of Equations** | **19** |
|    2.1 Solving the System | 20 |
|    2.2 System of Non-Linear Equations | 22 |
| **3 Indices, Logarithm, and Exponents** | **27** |
|    3.1 Indices | 28 |
|    3.2 Logarithm | 32 |
|    3.3 Solving Equations | 34 |
|    3.4 Exponential Function and Logarithmic Function | 40 |
| **4 Quadratics** | **47** |
|    4.1 Solving Quadratic Equation | 48 |
|    4.2 Maximum and Minimum | 53 |
|    4.3 Solving Quadratic Inequalities | 55 |
| **5 Remainder and Factor Theorem** | **61** |
|    5.1 Remainder Theorem | 62 |
|    5.2 Factor Theorem | 66 |
| **6 Matrices** | **69** |
|    6.1 Introduction to Matrix | 70 |

| | |
|---|---|
| 6.2 Addition, Subtraction, and Scalar Multiplication of Matrix | 71 |
| 6.3 Multiplication of Matrix | 73 |
| 6.4 Determinant and Inverse of $2 \times 2$ Matrix | 76 |

## 7 Coordinate Geometry — 79
- 7.1 Important Formulas … 80

## 8 Linear Law — 87
- 8.1 Linear Law … 88

## 9 Functions — 93
- 9.1 Essential Knowledge for Functions … 94
- 9.2 Quick Facts for Transformation … 96
- 9.3 Absolute-valued function … 99

## 10 Trigonometry — 105
- 10.1 Trigonometric Ratio … 106
- 10.2 Trigonometric Functions … 111
- 10.3 Transformation of Trigonometric Functions … 113
- 10.4 Other Trigonometric Functions … 115
- 10.5 Trigonometric Identities … 119
- 10.6 Trigonometric Equations … 123
- 10.7 Law of Sines and Law of Cosines … 125

## 11 Counting and Binomial Theorem — 133
- 11.1 Counting Principle … 134
- 11.2 Permutation and Combination … 136
- 11.3 The Binomial Expansion … 140

## 12 Differentiation — 145
- 12.1 Instantaneous Rate of Change … 146
- 12.2 Basic derivatives … 147
- 12.3 Differentiation Rules … 149
- 12.4 Tangent and Normal Lines … 151

## 13 Related Rates — 155
- 13.1 Rates of Change … 156
- 13.2 Related Rates … 157

13.3 Small Changes . . . . . . . . . . . . . . . . . . . . . . . . . . . . . 159

# 14 Higher-Derivatives **163**
  14.1 Meaning of First Derivative . . . . . . . . . . . . . . . . . . . . . 164
  14.2 Meaning of Second Derivative . . . . . . . . . . . . . . . . . . . . 166

# 15 Integration **169**
  15.1 Indefinite Integral . . . . . . . . . . . . . . . . . . . . . . . . . . 170
  15.2 Definite Integral . . . . . . . . . . . . . . . . . . . . . . . . . . . 175

# 16 Bounded Area **179**
  16.1 Vertical Slicing . . . . . . . . . . . . . . . . . . . . . . . . . . . . 180
  16.2 Horizontal Slicing . . . . . . . . . . . . . . . . . . . . . . . . . . 182

# 17 Kinematics **185**
  17.1 Motion on a Straight Line . . . . . . . . . . . . . . . . . . . . . . 186

# 18 Vectors **193**
  18.1 Geometric Vectors . . . . . . . . . . . . . . . . . . . . . . . . . . 194
  18.2 Coordinate Vectors . . . . . . . . . . . . . . . . . . . . . . . . . . 195
  18.3 Vector Algebra . . . . . . . . . . . . . . . . . . . . . . . . . . . . 196

# 19 Relative Velocity **201**
  19.1 True Velocity and Relative Velocity . . . . . . . . . . . . . . . . . 202
  19.2 Relative Motion in a Current or Air . . . . . . . . . . . . . . . . . 203
  19.3 Relative Motion of Two Moving Objects . . . . . . . . . . . . . . 206

# Topic 1

# Set Theory

- ✓ Types of Set
- ✓ Perform Basic Set Arithmetic
- ✓ Important Principles

## 1.1 Types of Set

A set is a well-defined collection of objects, and each object is called a *member* or *element* of the set. A set is denoted by a capital letter and is expressed by listing its elements, e.g. $V = \{a, e, i, o, u\}$. First of all, sets can be categorized by their sizes. If a set contains only a finite number of elements, we say "a set is finite." If not, we say "a set is infinite." For infinite sets, there are some famous examples one must know.

- $\mathbb{N}$: the set of natural numbers
- $\mathbb{Z}$: the set of integers
- $\mathbb{Q}$: the set of rational numbers
- $\mathbb{R}$: the set of real numbers
- $\mathbb{C}$: the set of complex numbers

$$\mathbb{N} \subset \mathbb{Z} \subset \mathbb{Q} \subset \mathbb{R} \subset \mathbb{C}$$

If a set is given to you, how would you write whether a specific element(or object) belongs to the set? Given a set $V = \{a, e, i, o, u\}$, we usually write $a$ is an element of $V$, i.e., $a \in V$. The sign, $\in$, is epsilon in Greek letter, commonly used for a set theory. Suppose we look for an element $b$. It is not included in $V$. Therefore, we write that $b$ is *not* included in $V$, i.e., $b \notin V$. This is formally called a negation(putting a vertical bar on the sign) of a relation.

There are other ways to write down a set, specifying a condition for elements. For instance, one can write $\{x : x \text{ is a prime number and } x < 30\}$. In short, we can express the previous set $V$ in two ways.

> **Two Types of Set Notations**
>
> There are two types of set notations, i.e.,
>
> - Element-specific method : $V = \{a, e, i, o, u\}$
> - Condition-specified method : $V = \{x \in \text{Alphabets} : x \text{ is a vowel}\}$.

## 1.2 Perform Basic Set Arithmetic

Most of the arithmetic operations we learn in this chapter are widely used for a finite set. For any finite set $P$, $n(P)$ (or $|P|$) indicates the number of elements in $P$. A *null* or *empty* set is denoted by $\{\}$ or $\emptyset$. For any two sets $P$ and $Q$, the following properties are satisfied.

- $P = Q$ if the two sets have same elements.
- $P \subseteq Q$ if $x \in P \implies x \in Q$.
- $P \cup Q = \{x : x \in P \text{ or } x \in Q\}$.
- $P \cap Q = \emptyset$ if and only if $P$ and $Q$ are disjoint sets.
- $P^c \cap Q^c = (P \cup Q)^c$ or $P^c \cup Q^c = (P \cap Q)^c$, known for De Morgan's Law.

These arithmetic rules are used when we find the minimum or maximum number of elements in a set $X \cap Y$, for instance. If $n(X) = 5$ and $n(Y) = 10$, then it is natural to think of $X \cap Y$ as a subset of $X$ and $Y$. Then, $X \cap Y \subset X$ or $X \cap Y \subset Y$. Hence, we can deduce that maximal possible of number of elements for $X \cap Y$ is reached when $X$ is a proper subset of $Y$. That is, $X$ is completely contained in $Y$. In this case, then $X \cap Y = X$, which means $n(X \cap Y) = n(X)$. This crucial observation is widely used in Additional Math question related to Set Theory.

For any set $P$ and universal set $\Omega$, we have the following properties satisfied, which are useful when we solve set-related questions. These properties appear due to the existence of complement sets. In mathematics, we count many things, i.e., the total number of cases when something happens or the probability of an event to occur. The usefulness of a complement set shines out when direct calculations are cumbersome.

- $P \subseteq \Omega$ and $0 \leq n(P) \leq n(\Omega)$.
- $P'$ or $P^c = \{x : x \in \Omega \text{ and } x \notin P\}$.
- $P \cap P' = \emptyset$.
- $P \cup P' = \Omega$.

## 1.3 Important Principles

There are two major principles when we deal with set-related questions. The first principle should be understood as the meaning of subtraction. In mathematics, we use subtraction when something is double-counted. In order to get rid of repetitive counts, subtraction is used.

**Inclusion-Exclusion Principle**

Given a universal set $U$, and subsets $A, B, C$, then the following equation holds true.

$$n(A \cup B \cup C) = n(A) + n(B) + n(C) - n(A \cap B) - n(A \cap C) - n(B \cap C) + n(A \cap B \cap C)$$

On the other hand, De Morgan's Law is used when it is easy to count complement set. This principle itself does not seem important in any way, but there are multiple questions that ask you to use the law.

**De Morgan's Law**

Given two sets $A, B$, then the following equations are valid.

$$n(A^c \cap B^c) = n((A \cup B)^c)$$
$$n(A^c \cup B^c) = n((A \cap B)^c)$$

**1** Given that $n(U) = 40, n(A) = 25, n(B) = 30$ and $n(A \cap B) = x$, find the least and greatest possible value of $x$.

### Example

If $A = \{1,2,3,4\}$ and $B = \{2,3,4,5\}$, what is $n(A \cup B)$?

**Solution**

Since $A \cup B = \{1,2,3,4,5\}$, $n(A \cup B) = 5$. Also, by the principle of inclusion and exclusion, $n(A \cup B) = n(A) + n(B) - n(A \cap B)$. Therefore, $4 + 4 - 3 = 5$.

$\boxed{2}$ Given that $n(U) = 55, n(A) = 28, n(B) = x$ and $n(A \cap B) = 5$, express, in terms of $x$, $n(A \cup B)$ and $n(A^c \cap B^c)$. Hence, find the greatest and the smallest possible values of $x$.

$\boxed{3}$ Given that $n(U) = 23, n(A \cap B) = x, n(A) = y, n(B) = 2y$ and $n(A^c \cap B^c) = 7$, find the least possible value of $y$.

> **Example**
>
> If the universal set $U = \{1,2,3,4,\cdots,10\}$, $A = \{1,2,3,4\}$ and $B = \{2,3,4,5\}$, what is $n(A^c \cap B^c)$?
>
> **Solution**
>
> $n(A^c \cap B^c) = n((A \cup B)^c) = n(U) - n(A \cup B) = 10 - 5 = 5$.

**4** Given that $n(U) = 50$, $n(P) = 28$, $n(Q) = 35$ and $n(P^c \cap Q^c) = x$, answer the following questions.

(a) Express $n(P^c \cap Q)$, $n(P \cap Q)$ and $n(P \cap Q^c)$ in terms of $x$.

(b) Find the greatest and the smallest possible values of $x$.

5. Out of 32 students in a class, 26 own desktop computers and 9 own laptop computers. It is given that

$$U = \{ \text{ students in the class } \}$$
$$A = \{ \text{ students who own a desktop computer } \}$$
$$B = \{ \text{ students who own a laptop computer } \}$$

If $n(A \cap B) = x$, then answer the following questions.

(a) Express $n(A^c \cap B^c)$ in terms of $x$.

(b) Find the smallest and largest possible values of $x$.

## Answerkey to Practice Problems

1. 15

2. 5, 32

3. 6

4. 0, 15

5. $x-3$, 3, 9

# Topic 2

# System of Equations

- ✓ Solving the System
- ✓ System of Non-Linear Equations

## 2.1 Solving the System

Simultaneous equations are the set of equations with more than one variable. When we look for a solution, we look for a pair that satisfies the given equations at the same time. Suppose there is a system of equations such as

$$\begin{cases} x+y=2 \\ 3x+y=4 \end{cases}$$

Then, we know that $(x,y) = (1,1)$ satisfies the two linear equations at the same time. We say, $(x,y) = (1,1)$ is a solution to the system.

Simultaneous linear equations, a.k.a, the system of linear equations, can be solved either by *substitution* or *elimination*.

---

**Technique of *substitution***

$$\begin{cases} 3x+5y=11 \\ 2x-3y=1 \end{cases}$$

The first equation gives $3x = 11-5y \implies x = \dfrac{11-5y}{3}$. Substituting it into the second equation, we have $\dfrac{22}{3} - \dfrac{10}{3}y - 3y = 1$. Therefore, we get $-\dfrac{19y}{3} = -\dfrac{19}{3} \implies y = 1$. In short, $x = \dfrac{11-5}{3} = 2$.

---

$\boxed{1}$ Solve the following system of equations by substitution.

$$\begin{cases} 4x-y=11 \\ 5x+2y=17 \end{cases}$$

**Technique of *elimination***

$$\begin{cases} 3x+5y=11 \\ 2x-3y=1 \end{cases}$$

If we multiply 2 to the first equation and 3 to the second equation, we have

$$\begin{cases} 6x+10y=22 \\ 6x-9y=3 \end{cases}$$

Subtracting both hand sides of the equations vertically, we get $19y=19 \implies y=1$. Substitute $y=1$ into the first equation to retrieve $x=2$.

**2** Solve the following system of equations by elimination.

$$\begin{cases} 2x-3y=10 \\ 5x-6y=25 \end{cases}$$

## 2.2 System of Non-Linear Equations

The following steps solve simultaneous linear and non-linear equations.

1. Rearrange one of the equations in one *unknown* and solve the equation.

2. Substitute the results from Step 1 into the linear equation to find the other *unknown*.

### Example

Solve $\begin{cases} y - 1 = x^2 + x \\ y - 2x = 3 \end{cases}$.

### Solution

Look at the second equation $y = 2x + 3$. Substitute $y$ into the first equation so that $2x + 2 = x^2 + x$. Therefore, we have $x^2 - x - 2 = (x-2)(x+1) = 0$, i.e., $x = 2$ or $x = -1$. In short, we have two solutions, $(x, y) = (2, 7)$ or $(-1, 1)$.

Note that there might be more than one solution pair $(x, y)$. The best strategy here is to find all values for one variable and substitute those values into one of the equation to find the corresponding values for the other variables.

**3** Solve the following system of equations.

$$\begin{cases} x + y = 9 \\ xy = 8 \end{cases}$$

**4** Find the coordinates of the points where the line meets the curve.

$$\begin{cases} 2x+3y=-1 \\ x(x-y)=2 \end{cases}$$

**5** Solve the equations

$$\begin{cases} x+2y=7 \\ x^2-4x+y^2=1 \end{cases}$$

**6** A line that passes through $(0,-1)$ meets the curve $x^2 - 4x + y^2 - 2y + 4 = 0$ at the point $(3,1)$. Find the coordinates of the second point where the line meets the curve.

**7** If the line $3x - 5y = 8$ meets the curve $\dfrac{3}{x} - \dfrac{1}{y} = 4$ at $M$ and $N$, find the coordinates of the midpoint of $MN$.

**8** If the sum of two numbers is 4 and the sum of their squares minus three times their product is 76, find the numbers.

**9** If $(1,p)$ is a solution of simultaneous equations,

$$\begin{cases} 12x^2 - 5y^2 = 7 \\ 2p^2x - 5y = 7 \end{cases}$$

find the value of $p$ and the other solution.

# Answerkey to Practice Problems

1. $(x,y) = (3,1)$.

2. $(x,y) = (5,0)$.

3. $(1,8), (8,1)$

4. $(1,1), (-\frac{26}{7}, \frac{15}{7})$

5. $x = 3, y = 2$

6. $x = \frac{21}{13}, y = \frac{1}{13}$

7. $(0, \frac{7}{10})$

8. $(6,-2), (-2,6)$

9. $p = -1$, $(-\frac{3}{2}, -2), (1,-1)$

# Topic 3

# Indices, Logarithm, and Exponents

✓ Indices

✓ Logarithm

✓ Solving Equations

✓ Exponential Function and Logarithmic Function

## 3.1 Indices

Index expression is given by $a^m$ where $a > 0$. The following list shows the properties of indices. Assume that $a > 0$ and $p, q$ are positive integers.

1. $a^0 = 1$
2. $a^{-p} = \dfrac{1}{a^p}$
3. $a^{\frac{1}{p}} = \sqrt[p]{a}$
4. $a^{\frac{q}{p}} = (\sqrt[p]{a})^q$

The following arithmetic rules for indices are useful. Memorize them by heart. Assume $a, b > 0$ and $m, n$ are rational numbers.

1. $a^m \cdot a^n = a^{m+n}$
2. $a^n \cdot b^n = (ab)^n$
3. $\dfrac{a^m}{a^n} = a^{m-n}$
4. $\dfrac{a^n}{b^n} = \left(\dfrac{a}{b}\right)^n$
5. $(a^m)^n = a^{mn}$

**1** If $3^{x+2} = y$, find the value of $3^x$ in terms of $y$.

### Example

If $2^{4-x} = 32$, find the value of $x$.

**Solution**

Since $2^{4-x} = 2^5$, then $4 - x = 5$. Hence, $x = -1$.

**2** If $3^{x+1} = 3^{-x+7}$, find the value of $x$.

### Example

If $m + 2n = 2$, find the value of $3^m \times 9^n$.

**Solution**

$3^m \times 9^n = 3^m \times 3^{2n} = 3^{m+2n} = 3^2 = 9$.

**3** If $2a - b = 4$, find the value of $\dfrac{9^a}{3^b}$.

### Example

Simplify $2^{3-x} = \dfrac{8}{2^x}$.

**Solution**

$2^{3-x} = \dfrac{2^3}{2^x} = \dfrac{8}{2^x}$.

**4** Show that $(8x^2)^{8-p}\left(\dfrac{1}{2x}\right)^p = 2^{24-4p}(x^{16-3p})$.

### Example

Simplify $\sqrt{12} + \sqrt{27}$.

**Solution**

$\sqrt{12} + \sqrt{27} = 2\sqrt{3} + 3\sqrt{3} = 5\sqrt{3}$.

**5** Simplify $4\sqrt{2} - \sqrt{8} + \sqrt{50}$.

## Example

Simplify $\dfrac{\sqrt{3}-\sqrt{2}}{\sqrt{3}+\sqrt{2}}$.

**Solution**

$$\dfrac{\sqrt{3}-\sqrt{2}}{\sqrt{3}+\sqrt{2}} = \dfrac{(\sqrt{3}-\sqrt{2})(\sqrt{3}-\sqrt{2})}{(\sqrt{3}+\sqrt{2})(\sqrt{3}-\sqrt{2})}$$
$$= \dfrac{3-2\sqrt{6}+2}{3-2}$$
$$= 5-2\sqrt{6}$$

**6** Simplify $\dfrac{3\sqrt{2}-4}{3\sqrt{2}+4}$ by rationalizing the denominator.

**7** Find the positive values of $x$ for which $9x^{\frac{2}{3}}+4x^{-\frac{2}{3}}=37$.

## 3.2 Logarithm

Given $a^x = b$ where $a > 0, a \neq 1$ and $b > 0$, then we have a logarithmic form.

$$a^x = b \longleftrightarrow \log_a b = x$$

The following lists shows the properties of logarithms.

**Logarithmic Properties**

- $\log_a b^n = n \log_a b$
- $\log_a b + \log_a c = \log_a bc$
- $\log_a b - \log_a c = \log_a \dfrac{b}{c}$
- $(\log_a b) \times (\log_c d) = (\log_a d)(\log_c d)$
- $\dfrac{\log_a b}{\log_a c} = \log_c b$
- $\log_{a^n} b^m = \dfrac{m}{n} \log_a b$

There are two common logarithms used over the course works in high school: common log and natural log. These two logarithms have a unique notation without writing the base.

**Common Logarithm and Natural Logarithm**

✓ $\log_{10} x = \log(x) = \lg(x)$  ✓ $\log_e x = \ln(x)$

Here, $e$ refers to Euler number, which is slightly bigger than 2. Definition of $e$ involves a limit process, which will not be covered in this coursework. Nevertheless, knowing that $e$ is bigger than 2 is quite useful when we graph the function $y = \ln(x)$.

**Example**

Simplify $\log(2) + \log(5)$ as much as possible.

**Solution**

$\log(2) + \log(5) = \log(10) = \log_{10}(10) = 1$.

**8** Evaluate each of the following in terms of $x$ and $y$ given $x = \log_2 3$ and $y = \log_2 5$.

(a) $\log_2 15$

(b) $\log_2(7.5)$

(c) $\log_3 2$

(d) $\log_3 15$

(e) $\log_4 9$

(f) $\log_5 6$

**9** If $\log 2 = m$, express $\log_8 5$ in terms of $m$. (In many IGCSE textbooks, $\log x$ is written as $\lg x$.)

## 3.3 Solving Equations

Given $a^x = b$ where $a > 0 (\neq 1)$ and $b > 0$, we can find a solution $x$.

1. If $b$ can be written as $a^n$, then

$$a^x = a^n \implies x = n$$

2. Otherwise, take logarithms on both sides, i.e.,

$$\log a^x = \log b \implies x = \frac{\log b}{\log a}$$

In order to decide when to use logarithm to solve a given equation, first look at whether the exponent contains a variable. If so, logarithm might take down the exponent to a constant multiple and make a linear equation, which is easier to solve.

Also, the wise choice of base might be helpful in simplifying an exponential equation. For instance, if $3^x = 10$, then it is better to take $\log_3(3^x) = \log_3(10)$ rather than $\log_5(3^x) = \log_5(10)$ (or any other base). Nevertheless, the nature of a solution retrieved from any choice of base does not change. In fact, it is simply rewriting answer in a different form.

$$x = \log_3(10) = \frac{\log_5(10)}{\log_5(3)}$$

### Example

If $\log(19x+5) = 2$, then find the value of $x$.

**Solution**

$\log(19x+5) = 2 \implies 19x+5 = 10^2 \implies 19x = 95 \implies x = 5$.

**10** Solve $2\log_5 x = \log_5 9$.

**Example**

Solve $\log(x) + \log(x+15) = 2$.

**Solution**

$\log(x) + \log(x+15) = \log(x(x+15)) = 2 \implies x(x+15) = 100 \implies x = 5.$

**11** Solve $\log_5(x+6) + \log_5(x+2) = 1$.

**12** Solve $\ln x = \ln(x+6) - \ln(x-4)$.

> **Example**
>
> If $3^{m+5} = 10$, find the value of $m$ in a single logarithm.
>
> **Solution**
>
> $3^{m+5} = 10 \implies m+5 = \log_3(10) \implies m = \log_3(10) - 5 = \log_3(\frac{10}{3^5}) = \log_3(\frac{10}{243}).$

**13** Solve $8 \cdot 2^x = 5$.

**14** Solve $2^{x-2} = 3^{3x+2}$.

> **Example**
>
> Solve the simultaneous equations $3^{x+y} = 9$ and $2^{x-y} = 1$.
>
> **Solution**
>
> Since $x+y = 2$ and $x-y = 0$, then $x = 1$ and $y = 1$.

**15** Solve the simultaneous equations $64(4^y) = 16^x$ and $3^y = 4(3^{x-2}) - 1$.

**16** Find the value of $x$ for which $x^{\frac{3}{2}} - 8x^{-\frac{3}{2}} = 7$.

## Example

If $\log(a^3b^2) = 5x$ and $\log(\frac{a}{b^3}) = 2x$, find the value of $\log_a b$.

### Solution

$$\begin{cases} 3\log(a) + 2\log(b) = 5x \\ \log(a) - 3\log(b) = 2x \end{cases} \implies \log(a) = \frac{19x}{11} \text{ and } \log(b) = -\frac{x}{11}$$

$$\implies \log_a(b) = \frac{\log(b)}{\log(a)} = -\frac{1}{19}.$$

**17** Solve the equation $\log(3^x - 2^{4-x}) = 2 + \frac{1}{3}\log 8 - \frac{1}{4}x\log 16$.

**18** Find the exact value of $x$ if $(3x)^{\log 3} = (4x)^{\log 4}$.

### Example

Solve $2^{2x} - 2^x - 2 = 0$ for $x$.

**Solution**

$$2^{2x} - 2^x - 2 = 0$$
$$(2^x - 2)(2^x + 1) = 0$$
$$2^x = 2 \text{ and } -1$$
$$x = 1$$

**19** Solve $4^x - 3^{x+\frac{1}{2}} = 3^{x-\frac{1}{2}} - 2^{2x-1}$.

# 3.4 Exponential Function and Logarithmic Function

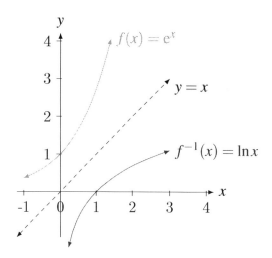

Exponential function and logarithmic function are inverse to one another. The properties of inverse function will be outlined in a different chapter. Nonetheless, it is important to analyze the graphs. First, exponential function is always above the *x*-axis, unless it is shifted downward. Likewise, logarithmic function is placed in the right side of the *y*-axis. Both graphs are those of increasing functions.

### Preventing Mistakes

1. $e^0 = 1$

2. $e^x > 0$ for all $x$

3. $\ln(1) = 0$

4. $\ln(0)$ does not exist. In fact, it goes toward $-\infty$.

These pieces of information are not limited to $e^x$ and $\ln(x)$. They are all applicable to other bases. Furthermore, the value of base is crucial when determining the shape of the function. Interestingly, the base value changes the shape of both functions. Both functions are one-to-one function such that each function is inverse to one another. They are either strictly increasing or decreasing depending on the base value.

1. $(\frac{1}{2})^x$ is decreasing.

2. $\log_{\frac{1}{2}}(x)$ is also decreasing.

3. $2^x$ is increasing

4. $\log_2(x)$ is also increasing.

**20** Sketch the graph of exponential function.

(a) $f(x) = 3^x$ 

(b) $f(x) = (\frac{1}{3})^x$

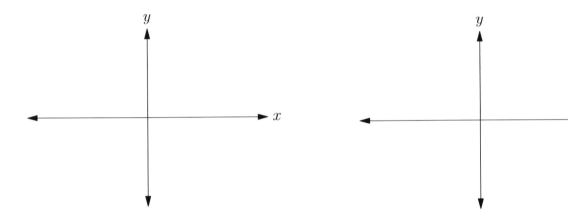

### Example

Find the range of $y = 2^{3-x} - 3$.

**Solution**

Since $2^{3-x} > 0$, then $y = 2^{3-x} - 3 > -3$. Therefore, the range is $(-3, \infty)$.

**21** Determine the domain, range, and horizontal asymptote of $f(x) = 3^x - 2$.

**22** Sketch the graph of $f(x) = -e^{3-x}$ and state the domain, range, and horizontal asymptote.

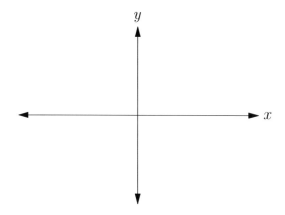

**23** Find the domain of the following logarithmic function.

(a) $f(x) = \log_2(3x+4)$

(b) $g(x) = \log_3 \dfrac{2-x}{x+2}$

(c) $h(x) = \log_{10}|x-3|$

# Answerkey to Practice Problems

1. $\dfrac{y}{9}$

2. 3

3. 81

4. $(8x^2)^{8-p}(\dfrac{1}{2x})^p = (2^3)^{8-p}(x^2)^{8-p}2^{-p}x^{-p} = 2^{24-3p}2^{-p} \times x^{16-2p}x^{-p} = 2^{24-4p}x^{16-3p}.$

5. $7\sqrt{2}$

6. $17 - 12\sqrt{2}$

7. $x = \dfrac{1}{27}, \dfrac{1}{8}$

8.

(a) $x+y$

(b) $x+y-1$

(c) $\dfrac{1}{x}$

(d) $\dfrac{y}{x}+1$

(e) $x$

(f) $\dfrac{x+1}{y}$

9. $\dfrac{1-m}{3m}$

10. $x = 3$

11. $x = -1$

12. $x = 6$

13. $x = \log_2 5 - 3$

14. $x = \dfrac{\ln 36}{\ln 2 - \ln 27}$

**15.** $(2,1), (1,-1)$

**16.** $x = 4$

**17.** $x = 3$

**18.** $x = \dfrac{1}{12}$

**19.** $x = \dfrac{3}{2}$

**20.**

(a)  (b)

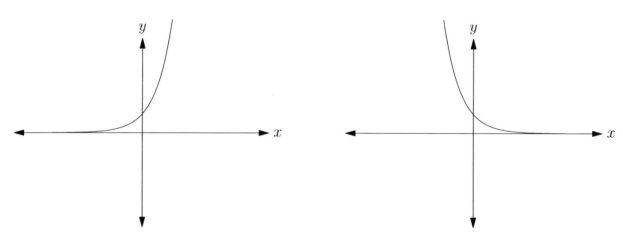

**21.** Domain is the set of all real numbers; range is $\{y \in \mathbb{R} | y > -2\}$; horizontal asymptote is $y = -2$.

**22.**

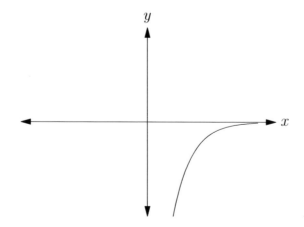

Domain is the set of all real numbers, range is $\{y \in \mathbb{R} | y < 0\}$; horizontal asymptote is $y = 0$.

**23.**

(a) $x > -\dfrac{4}{3}$

(b) $-2 < x < 2$

(c) $x \neq 3$

# Topic 4

# Quadratics

✓ Solving Quadratic Equations

✓ Maximum and Minimum

✓ Solving Quadratic Inequalities

# 4.1 Solving Quadratic Equation

1. Factorization

$$ax^2 + bx + c = a(x-m)(x-n)$$

2. Completion of Squares

$$ax^2 + bx + c = a(x-p)^2 + q$$

3. Quadratic Formula

$$x = \frac{-b \pm \sqrt{b^2 - 4ac}}{2a} \text{ for } ax^2 + bx + c = 0$$

4. Vieta's Formula

For $\alpha, \beta$, roots of the equation $ax^2 + bx + c = 0$,

$$\alpha + \beta = -\frac{b}{a} \text{ and } \alpha\beta = \frac{c}{a}$$

### Example

Complete the square for $4x^2 + 6x + 1$.

### Solution

$$4x^2 + 6x + 1 = 4(x^2 + \frac{3}{2}x) + 1$$
$$= 4(x^2 + \frac{3}{2}x + \frac{9}{16}) - \frac{9}{4} + 1$$
$$= 4(x + \frac{3}{4})^2 - \frac{5}{4}$$

**1** The equation of a curve is given by $y = x^2 + ax + 3$, where $a$ is a constant. Given that this equation can also be written as $y = (x+4)^2 + b$, find the value of $a$ and of $b$.

## Graph of $f(x) = ax^2 + bx + c$

As shown in the figure, the graph is a parabola. If $a > 0$, then the parabola has its minimum. If $a < 0$, then the parabola has its maximum.

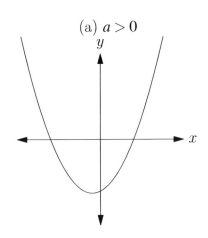
(a) $a > 0$

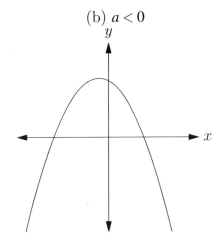
(b) $a < 0$

## Types of roots of $ax^2 + bx + c = 0$

The discriminant for $ax^2 + bx + c = 0$ is $D = b^2 - 4ac$.

### Discriminant

1. $D > 0$: the equation has two distinct real solutions (with no complex solution)

2. $D = 0$: the equation has one real solution (with no complex solution)

3. $D < 0$: the equation has no real solution (but two complex solutions)

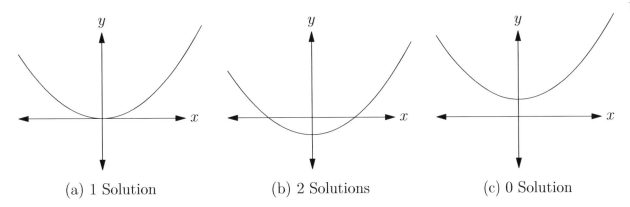

(a) 1 Solution      (b) 2 Solutions      (c) 0 Solution

As one can see from the three graphs above, the graph has one $x$-intercept if the discriminant is 0. Likewise, the graph has two $x$-intercepts if the discriminant is positive. Lastly, the graph has no $x$-intercept if the discriminant is negative.

> **Example**
>
> Determine the value of $k$ if $x^2 + kx + (k-1) = 0$ has one real solution.
>
> **Solution**
>
> $k^2 - 4(k-1) = 0 \implies k^2 - 4k + 4 = 0 \implies k = 2.$

**2** Find the set of values of $k$ for which the equation $x^2 + (k-2)x + (2k-4) = 0$ has real roots.

**3** For what values of $k$ will the $x$-axis be tangent to the curve $y = kx^2 + x + kx + k$?

**4** It is given that $f(x) = 4x^2 + kx + k$. Solve the following questions.

(a) Find the set of values of $k$ for which the equation $f(x) = 3$ has no real roots.

Assume that $k = 10$.

(b) Express $f(x)$ in the form $(ax+b)^2 + c$.

(c) Find the least value of $f(x)$ and the value of $x$ for which this least value occurs.

> **Example**
>
> If $r$ and $s$ are solutions to $x^2 - 4x - 4 = 0$, what is the value of $r^2 + s^2$?
>
> **Solution**
>
> Since $r + s = 4$ and $rs = -4$, then $r^2 + s^2 = (r+s)^2 - 2rs = 16 - 2(-4) = 24$.

**5** The roots of the quadratic equation $x^2 - \sqrt{20}x + 2 = 0$ are $c$ and $d$. Without using a calculator, show that
$$\frac{1}{c} + \frac{1}{d} = \sqrt{5}$$

## 4.2 Maximum and Minimum

Given $ax^2+bx+c$, the vertex(a turning point) is located at $x=-\dfrac{b}{2a}$.

(1) $a>0 \implies f(-\dfrac{b}{2a})$ is minimum

(2) $a<0 \implies f(-\dfrac{b}{2a})$ is maximum

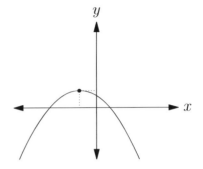

As one can notice from the two graphs above, the line $x=-\dfrac{b}{2a}$ for $y=ax^2+bx+c$ is the line of symmetry, and the point of intersection between the line of symmetry and the graph of $y=ax^2+bx+c$ is either maximum or minimum value, depending on the sign of $a$.

**6** The function $f$ is given by $f(x)=2x^2-8x+5$. Show that

$$f(x)=2(x+a)^2+b$$

where $a$ and $b$ are to be found.

**7** Sketch the curve $y = |x^2 - x - 2|$.

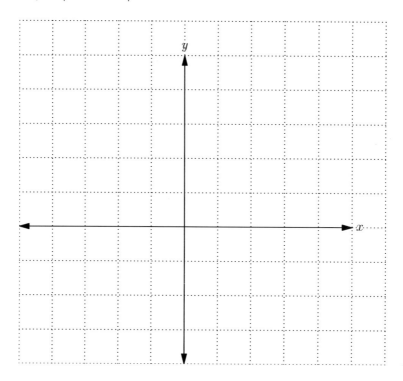

**8** Find the range of $f(x) = x^2 - 3x - 4$ for the domain $-1 \leq x \leq 4$.

## 4.3 Solving Quadratic Inequalities

For $D > 0$ and $a > 0$ for $f(x) = ax^2 + bx + c$, assume the two distinct $x$-intercepts are $\alpha$ and $\beta$ where $\alpha < \beta$. Then we have the following results.

$$y = a(x - \alpha)(x - \beta)$$

1. $x < \alpha \implies f(x) > 0$

2. $\alpha < x < \beta \implies f(x) < 0$

3. $\beta < x \implies f(x) > 0$

The following figure shows the nature of this inequality.

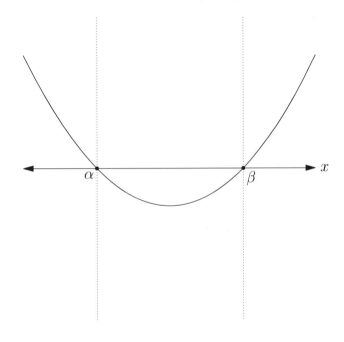

As one can check easily from the figure,

- The portions of the graph of $y = a(x - \alpha)(x - \beta)$ are below the $x$-axis $=$ $(x - \alpha)(x - \beta) < 0 = \alpha < x < \beta$.

- The portions of the graph of $y = a(x - \alpha)(x - \beta)$ are above the $x$-axis $=$ $(x - \alpha)(x - \beta) > 0 = x < \alpha$ or $\beta < x$.

On the other hand, for $D > 0$ and $a < 0$, then the results are reversed.

$$y = a(x - \alpha)(x - \beta)$$

1. $x < \alpha \implies f(x) < 0$

2. $\alpha < x < \beta \implies f(x) > 0$

3. $\beta < x \implies f(x) < 0$

The following figure also captures the nature of this inequality.

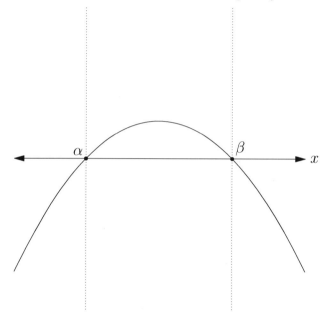

Similar to the previous case,

- The portions of the graph of $y = a(x - \alpha)(x - \beta)$ are below the $x$-axis $= (x - \alpha)(x - \beta) > 0 = \alpha < x < \beta$.

- The portions of the graph of $y = a(x - \alpha)(x - \beta)$ are above the $x$-axis $= (x - \alpha)(x - \beta) < 0 = x < \alpha$ or $\beta < x$.

This corresponds to the sign analysis using algebraic tools. For instance, if $y = a(x - \alpha)(x - \beta)$ where $a < 0$ and $\alpha < \beta$, then

- If $x < \alpha$, then $x - \alpha < 0$ and $x - \beta < 0$, so $a(x - \alpha)(x - \beta) = (-)(-)(-) < 0$.

- If $\alpha < x < \beta$, then $x - \alpha > 0$ and $x - \beta < 0 <$ so $a(x - \alpha)(x - \beta) = (-)(+)(-) > 0$.

- If $\beta < x$, then $x - \alpha > 0$ and $x - \beta > 0$, so $a(x - \alpha)(x - \beta) = (+)(+)(+) > 0$.

**9** Find the value of $a$ and $b$ for which the solution set of the quadratic inequality $x^2 + ax > b$ is $\{x : x > 2\} \cup \{x : x < -4\}$.

**10** Find the solution set of the quadratic inequality.

(a) $x^2 - 8x + 12 < 0$  (b) $x^2 - 8x < 0$

(c) Hence, find the solution set of the inequality $|x^2 - 8x + 6| < 6$.

# Answerkey to Practice Problems

1. $a = 8, b = -13$

2. $k \geq 2$ or $10 \geq k$

3. $-\dfrac{1}{3}, 1$

4. 

(a) $\{4 < k < 12\}$

(b) $a = 2, b = \dfrac{5}{2}, c = \dfrac{5}{4}$

(c) $f(x) = \dfrac{15}{4}, x = -\dfrac{5}{4}$

5. Since $cd = 2$ and $c + d = \sqrt{20}$, $\dfrac{1}{c} + \dfrac{1}{d} = \dfrac{c+d}{cd} = \dfrac{\sqrt{20}}{2} = \sqrt{5}$.

6. $a = -2, b = -3$

7.

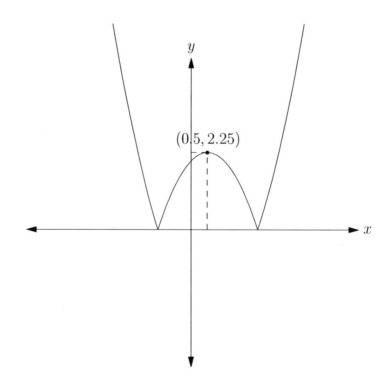

8. $-\dfrac{25}{4} \geq y \geq 0$

**9.** $a = 2, b = 8$

**10.**

(a) $2 < x < 6$

(b) $0 < x < 8$

(c) $0 < x < 2$ or $6 < x < 8$

# Topic 5

# Remainder and Factor Theorem

✓ Remainder Theorem

✓ Factor Theorem

## 5.1 Remainder Theorem

First, we can apply long division on polynomials.

$$
\begin{array}{r}
x^2+x+7\phantom{000000} \\
x-3 \overline{\smash{)}\, x^3-2x^2+4x-3} \\
\underline{x^3-3x^2\phantom{0000000}} \\
x^2+4x\phantom{000} \\
\underline{x^2-3x\phantom{000}} \\
7x-3 \\
\underline{7x-21} \\
18
\end{array}
$$

**Analysis**

1. $x-3$ is a divisor.

2. $x^2+x+7$ is a quotient.

3. $x^3-2x^2+4x-3$ is a dividend

4. 18 is a remainder

On the other hand, we can compute the remainder directly. This is the remainder theorem. If $p(x)$ is divided by $x-a$, then the remainder is $p(a)$.

$$p(x) = (x-a)q(x)+r$$
$$p(a) = (a-a)q(a)+r$$
$$p(a) = 0+r$$
$$p(a) = r$$

**1** The expression $6x^3 + ax^2 - (a+1)x + b$ has a remainder of 15 when divided by $x+2$ and a remainder of 24 when divided by $x+1$. Show that $a = 8$ and find the value of $b$.

---

### Example

If $f(x) = x^3 + 3x^2 + 3x + 1$, what is the value of $f(-1)$? Hence, determine whether $x+1$ is a factor of $f(x)$.

**Solution**

$f(-1) = -1 + 3 - 3 + 1 = 0$, so $x+1$ is a factor of $f(x)$.

---

**2** It is given that $x-1$ is a factor of $f(x)$, where $f(x) = x^3 - 6x^2 + ax + b$.

(a) Express $b$ in terms of $a$.

(b) Show that the remainder when $f(x)$ is divided by $x-3$ is twice the remainder when $f(x)$ is divided by $x-2$.

**3** Given $f(x) = x^3 + mx^2 + nx - 3$, when $f(x)$ is divided by $x-1$ and $x+1$, the remainders are 1 and $-9$, respectively. Find the values of $m$ and $n$.

**4** When the polynomial $g(x) = m(x-1)^2 + n(x+2)^2$ is divided by $x+1$ and $x-2$, the remainders are 3 and $-15$, respectively. Find the values of $m$ and $n$.

**5** When the polynomials $x^3 - 4x + 3$ and $x^3 - x^2 + x + 9$ are divided by $x - m$, the remainders are equal. Find the possible values of *m*.

## 5.2 Factor Theorem

**Factor Theorem**

If $mx+n$ is a factor of $f(x)$, then $f(-\frac{n}{m})=0$, and vice versa.

**6** The remainder when $x(x+b)(x-2b)$ is divided by $x-b$ is $-16$. Find the value of $b$.

**7** Solve the following questions.

(a) Show that $2x-1$ is a factor of $2x^3 - 5x^2 + 10x - 4$.

(b) Hence, show that $2x^3 - 5x^2 + 10x - 4 = 0$ has only one real root and state the value of this root.

> **Example**
>
> Determine whether $x-1$ is a factor of $x^3+4x^2-6x+1$.
>
> **Solution**
>
> If we substitute $x=1$ into the expression $x^3+4x-6x+1$, then $1^3+4(1)^2-6(1)+1=0$. Hence, $x-1$ must be its factor.

**8** Solve $2x^3-3x^2-11x+6=0$ for $x$.

# Answerkey for Practice Problems

1. $b = 13$

2. 

(a) $b = -a + 5$

(b) $f(3) = 27 - 6(9) + 3a + b = -27 + 3a + (-a + 5) = 2a - 22$ and
$f(2) = 8 - 6(4) + 2a + b = -16 + 2a + (-a + 5) = a - 11$. Hence, $f(3) = 2f(2)$.

3. $m = -1, n = 4$

4. $m = 1, n = -1$

5. $m = 6$ or $-1$

6. $b = 2$

7. 

(a) $f(\frac{1}{2}) = 2(\frac{1}{8}) - 5(\frac{1}{4}) + 10(\frac{1}{2}) - 4 = -1 + 5 - 4 = 0$.

(b) Since $2x^3 - 5x^2 + 10x - 4 = (2x - 1)(x^2 - 2x + 4)$ and $x^2 - 2x + 4 = 0$ has no real solution because the discriminant is $(-2)^2 - 4(4) < 0$. Hence, there is one real solution $x = \frac{1}{2}$.

8. $x = \frac{1}{2}, 3, -2$

# Topic 6

# Matrices

✓ Introduction to Matrix

✓ Addition, Subtraction, and Scalar Multiplication of Matrix

✓ Multiplication of Matrix

✓ Determinant and Inverse of $2 \times 2$ Matrix

## 6.1 Introduction to Matrix

Matrix is an array of numbers in rows and columns. There are some vocabularies we should know in order to understand what a matrix actually is.

- Order(or dimension) of a matrix : given $m$ number of rows and $n$ number of columns, the matrix has $m \times n$ dimension. Suppose there is a $2 \times 3$ matrix $A$, then denote each entry with subscripts of row and column at which it is placed.

$$\begin{bmatrix} x_{11} & x_{12} & x_{13} \\ x_{21} & x_{22} & x_{23} \end{bmatrix} = A_{2 \times 3}$$

- Two matrices with equal dimension are equal if and only if all entries are equal.

$$\begin{bmatrix} x_{11} & x_{12} \\ x_{21} & x_{22} \end{bmatrix} = \begin{bmatrix} w_{11} & w_{12} \\ w_{21} & w_{22} \end{bmatrix} \implies x_{11} = w_{11}, x_{12} = w_{12}, x_{21} = w_{21}, x_{22} = w_{22}$$

**1** A drinks stall sold 160 cups of coffee, 125 cups of tea and 210 glasses of soft drinks on Monday. On Tuesday, it sold 145 cups of coffee, 130 cups of tea and 275 glasses of soft drinks. On Wednesday, it sold 120 cups of coffee, 155 cups of tea and 325 glasses of soft drinks. Design a matrix to represent this information, labeling the rows and columns. State the order of the matrix.

## 6.2 Addition, Subtraction, and Scalar Multiplication of Matrix

We can perform matrix addition or subtraction, or multiply a scalar(or a number) to a given matrix if the dimension is same.

- Addition or Subtraction: Given two matrices, we add or subtract elements at each entry. Note that only the two matrices of equal dimension can be added or subtracted.

$$\begin{bmatrix} x_{11} & x_{12} & x_{13} \\ x_{21} & x_{22} & x_{23} \end{bmatrix} \pm \begin{bmatrix} y_{11} & y_{12} & y_{13} \\ y_{21} & y_{22} & y_{23} \end{bmatrix} = \begin{bmatrix} x_{11} \pm y_{11} & x_{12} \pm y_{12} & x_{13} \pm y_{13} \\ x_{21} \pm y_{21} & x_{22} \pm y_{22} & x_{23} \pm y_{23} \end{bmatrix}$$

- Scalar multiplication: Given a matrix and a scalar(=number), we have a scalar multiple as

$$k \begin{bmatrix} y_{11} & y_{12} & y_{13} \\ y_{21} & y_{22} & y_{23} \end{bmatrix} = \begin{bmatrix} ky_{11} & ky_{12} & ky_{13} \\ ky_{21} & ky_{22} & ky_{23} \end{bmatrix}$$

**2** The list prices, in dollars, of "ten-year series" for these subjects from two publishers are shown below.

|   | Math  | English | Literature | Korean |
|---|-------|---------|------------|--------|
| A | 10.30 | 25.10   | 15.20      | 10.00  |
| B | 9.90  | 28.30   | 15.30      | 11.50  |

Represent the information contained in the table as a matrix $M$. These publishers sell them to a bookshop at 15% discount. Find the matrix $D$ that represents the discounted prices, given to the bookshop.

3. If $A = \begin{bmatrix} 0 & 0 \\ 1 & 1 \end{bmatrix}, B = \begin{bmatrix} 1 & 0 \\ 1 & 1 \end{bmatrix}$, then find the sum of all entries for $2A + B$.

4. Given $A = \begin{bmatrix} 2 & 0 \\ 1 & 0 \end{bmatrix}, B = \begin{bmatrix} x & 0 \\ 2 & -3 \end{bmatrix}$, if the sum of all entries for $A + B$ is 6, find the value of $x$.

## 6.3 Multiplication of Matrix

Given two matrices $A_{m\times n}$ and $B_{n\times p}$, then $AB$ has the dimension of $m \times p$. The usual rule for row-column multiplication can be illustrated by the following. Suppose there is a $X_{2\times 3}, Y_{3\times 2}$ and $XY_{2\times 2}$. Then, the entry at the $i$th row and the $j$th column of $XY$ is computed by a dot product of the $i$th row of $X$ and the $j$th column of $Y$. For instance, the dot product of the first row of $X$ and the first column of $Y$ results in $z_{11}$.

$$\begin{bmatrix} x_{11} & x_{12} & x_{13} \\ \dots & \dots & \dots \end{bmatrix} \times \begin{bmatrix} y_{11} & \dots \\ y_{21} & \dots \\ y_{31} & \dots \end{bmatrix} = \begin{bmatrix} z_{11} & \dots \\ \dots & \dots \end{bmatrix}$$

**5** A cafe sells an Ice Americano and an Ice Latte, each in small or large glasses. The cost of a small glass of either drink is $2.00 and the cost of large glass is $3.5. During a period of twenty minutes, the following number of glasses of drink were sold.

|  | Small | Large |
|---|---|---|
| Americano | 6 | 2 |
| Latte | 5 | 1 |

Given that $X = \begin{bmatrix} 6 & 2 \\ 5 & 1 \end{bmatrix}$ and $Y = \begin{bmatrix} 2.00 \\ 3.50 \end{bmatrix}$, find $XY$ and explain what the numbers in $XY$ represent.

**6** Given that $A = \begin{bmatrix} 1 & 1 \\ 0 & 0 \end{bmatrix}$ find $A^{23}$.

**7** If $A = \begin{bmatrix} 0 & 1 \\ 1 & 0 \end{bmatrix}, B = \begin{bmatrix} 1 & 1 \\ 0 & 1 \end{bmatrix}$, find $A^2B - A$.

8. Given two $2 \times 2$ matrices $M, N$ satisfying $M = \begin{bmatrix} 2 & -4 \\ -1 & 2 \end{bmatrix}, N = \begin{bmatrix} 1 & 2 \\ 2 & 4 \end{bmatrix}$, find $\frac{1}{3}MN - NM$.

9. Given $X = \begin{bmatrix} 1 & 1 \\ 1 & 0 \end{bmatrix}, Y = \begin{bmatrix} 1 & 2 \\ 3 & 4 \end{bmatrix}$, if $2X + A = XY$, then find a matrix $A$.

## 6.4 Determinant and Inverse of $2 \times 2$ Matrix

1. Identity Matrix : Identity matrix, known as $E_{2\times 2}$ (or $I_{2\times 2}$), is $\begin{bmatrix} 1 & 0 \\ 0 & 1 \end{bmatrix}$. Here, the principal diagonal is all 1's.

$$AI = IA_{2\times 2} = A_{2\times 2}$$

2. Inverse Matrix : Given $A_{2\times 2} = \begin{bmatrix} a & b \\ c & d \end{bmatrix}$, the inverse matrix $A^{-1}$ is equal to

$$\frac{1}{ad-bc} \begin{bmatrix} d & -a \\ -c & b \end{bmatrix}$$

where $ad - bc$ is the determinant of the matrix. If the determinant is 0, we say $A$ is singular(=not invertible). Otherwise, $A$ is invertible. Hence, $AA^{-1} = A^{-1}A = I$.

**10** Find the sum of all entries for $A^{-1}$ if $A = \begin{bmatrix} 1 & -2 \\ 0 & 1 \end{bmatrix}$.

**11** Find the value of a natural number $n$ if all of the entries of the inverse of $M = \begin{bmatrix} 2n & -7 \\ -1 & n \end{bmatrix}$ are natural numbers.

**12** Find the sum of entries for $X$ if $A = \begin{bmatrix} 1 & 2 \\ 2 & 5 \end{bmatrix}, B = \begin{bmatrix} 2 & -3 \\ 1 & -2 \end{bmatrix}$ and $AX = B$.

# Amswerkey to Practice Problems

1. $\begin{bmatrix} 160 & 125 & 210 \\ 145 & 130 & 275 \\ 120 & 155 & 325 \end{bmatrix} \begin{bmatrix} c \\ t \\ s \end{bmatrix}$

2. $0.85 \begin{bmatrix} 10.30 & 25.10 & 15.20 & 10.00 \\ 9.90 & 28.30 & 15.30 & 11.50 \end{bmatrix}$

3. 10

4. 4

5. $\begin{bmatrix} 6 & 2 \\ 5 & 1 \end{bmatrix} \begin{bmatrix} 2 \\ 3.5 \end{bmatrix} = \begin{bmatrix} 19 \\ 13.5 \end{bmatrix}$

6. $\begin{bmatrix} 1 & 1 \\ 0 & 0 \end{bmatrix}$

7. $\begin{bmatrix} 1 & 0 \\ -1 & 1 \end{bmatrix}$

8. $\begin{bmatrix} -2 & -4 \\ 1 & 2 \end{bmatrix}$

9. $\begin{bmatrix} 2 & 4 \\ -1 & 2 \end{bmatrix}$

10. 4

11. 2

12. $-2$

# Topic 7

# Coordinate Geometry

✓ Important Formulas

## 7.1 Important Formulas

- Midpoint formula : Given $(x_1,y_1)$ and $(x_2,y_2)$, the midpoint is given by

$$(\frac{x_1+x_2}{2}, \frac{y_1+y_2}{2})$$

- Distance formula : Given $(x_1,y_1)$ and $(x_2,y_2)$, the distance between the two points is

$$\sqrt{(x_1-x_2)^2+(y_1-y_2))^2}$$

> **Example**
>
> If $A$, $B$ and $C$ are collinear and $AB:BC = 2:3$, find the coordinates of $B$ if $A = (1,3)$ and $C = (6,-2)$.
>
> **Solution**
> Let $B = (x,y)$. Then, let's find out the $x$-coordinate by using the proportion equation.
>
> $$AB:BC = (x-1):(6-x)$$
> $$2:3 = (x-1):(6-x)$$
> $$3(x-1) = 2(6-x)$$
> $$3x-3 = 12-2x$$
> $$5x = 15$$
> $$x = 3$$
>
> Likewise, for the $y$-coordinate, we use the following proportion equation.
>
> $$AB:BC = (y-3):(-2-y)$$
> $$2:3 = (y-3):(-2-y)$$
> $$3(y-3) = 2(-2-y)$$
> $$3y-9 = -4-2y$$
> $$5y = -5$$
> $$y = -1$$
>
> Hence, $(x,y) = (3,-1)$.

The following lists show important formulas for lines in coordinate geometry.

- Gradient of line passing through $(x_1, y_1)$ and $(x_2, y_2)$ is $\dfrac{y_2 - y_1}{x_2 - x_1}$.

- Parallel lines have equal gradients.

- Three points $A, B, C$ are collinear if the gradient of $AB$ equals the gradient of $BC$.

- Two lines are perpendicular if the product of slopes is $-1$.

- Slope-point form : $y - y_1 = m(x - x_1)$.

- Slope-intercept form: $y = mx + b$.

### Example

If $A$, $B$ and $C$ are collinear and $AB : BC = 4 : 3$, find the coordinates of $C$ if $A = (1, 3)$ and $B = (5, -1)$.

**Solution**

Let $C = (x, y)$. Then, the proportion equation for $x$ implies

$$AB : BC = (5 - 1) : (x - 5)$$
$$4 : 3 = 4 : (x - 5)$$
$$3 = x - 5$$
$$x = 8$$

Likewise, the equation for $y$ implies

$$AB : BC = (-1 - 3) : (y - (-1))$$
$$4 : 3 = -4 : (y + 1))$$
$$-3 = y + 1$$
$$-4 = y$$

Hence, $(x, y) = (8, -4)$.

**1**

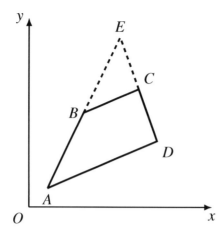

The diagram, which is not drawn to scale, shows a trapezium *ABCD* in which *BC* is parallel to *AD*. The side *AD* is perpendicular to *DC*. Point *A* is $(1,2)$, *B* is $(4,11)$ and *D* is $(17,10)$. Find

(a) the coordinates of *C*.

The lines *AB* and *DC* are extended to meet at *E*. Find

(b) the coordinates of *E*.

(c) the ratio of the area of triangle *EBC* to the area of trapezium *ABCD*.

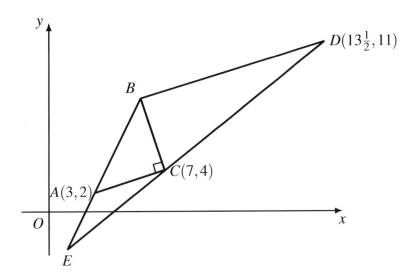

The diagram shows a triangle $ABC$ in which $A$ is the point $(3,2)$, $C$ is the point $(7,4)$ and angle $ACB = 90°$. The line $BD$ is parallel to $AC$ and $D$ is the point $(13\frac{1}{2}, 11)$. The lines $BA$ and $DC$ are extended to meet at $E$. Find

(a) the coordinates of $B$.

(b) the ratio of the area of the quadrilateral $ABDC$ to the area of the triangle $EBD$.

3

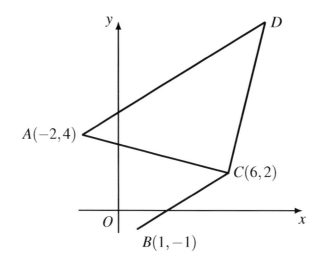

In the diagram the points A, B and C have coordinates $(-2,4), (1,-1)$ and $(6,2)$, respectively. The line AD is parallel to BC and $\angle ACD = 90°$.

(a) Find the equations of AD and CD.

(b) Find the coordinates of D.

(c) Show that $\triangle ACD$ is isosceles.

**4** The diagram, which is not drawn to scale, shows a right-angled triangle *ABC*, where *A* is the point $(6,11)$ and *B* is the point $(8,8)$. The point $D(5,6)$ is the mid-point of *BC*. The line *DE* is parallel to *AC* and $\angle DEC$ is a right-angle. Find the area of the entire figure *ABDECA*.

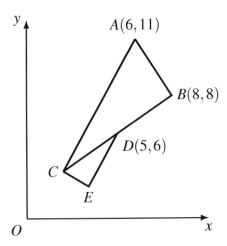

# Answerkey to Practice Problems

1.

(a) $(14, 16)$

(b) $(9, 26)$

(c) $25 : 39$

2.

(a) $B(\frac{11}{2}, 7)$

(b) $1 : 3$

3.

(a) $AD : y = \frac{3}{5}(x+2)+4$, $CD : 4(x-6)+2$

(b) $(8, 10)$

(c) $CD = \sqrt{(8-6)^2 + (10-2)^2} = \sqrt{68}$ and $AC = \sqrt{(-2-6)^2 + (2-4)^2} = \sqrt{68}$, so $AC = CD$. Hence, $\triangle ACD$ is isosceles.

4. $\dfrac{78}{5}$

# Topic 8

# Linear Law

✓ Linear Law

# 8.1 Linear Law

- Linear Law for Linear Equations

    For two variables $X$ and $Y$ related by $Y = mX + c$, the graph is a straight line with a gradient of $m$ and a $y$-intercept of $c$. The values of $m$ and $c$ are

    (a) calculated if two points are given.

    (b) estimated if the table is given.

- Linear Law for Non-Linear Equations In order to apply the linear law for non-linear equations, we should express the equation in the form

$$Y = mX + c$$

    where $Y, X$ are expressions with respect to $x$ and $y$.

    (a) The expressions for $X$ and $Y$ are explicitly given.

    (b) The expressions for $X$ and $Y$ are specified but not explicity given.

**1**

| $x$ | 2 | 3 | 4 | 5 | 6 |
|---|---|---|---|---|---|
| $y$ | 9.2 | 8.8 | 9.4 | 10.4 | 11.6 |

The table above shows experimental values of the variables $x$ and $y$. Then,

(a) express $y$ in terms of $x$.

(b) find the value of $x$ for which $x = \dfrac{45}{y}$.

**2**

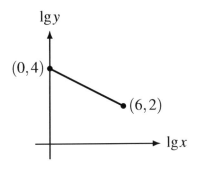

(a) Find lg(y) in terms of lg(x).

(b) Hence, find y in terms of x.

(c) Find the value of x when y = 700.

**3**

| $x$ | 1 | 2 | 3 | 4 | 5 |
|---|---|---|---|---|---|
| $y$ | $-1.5$ | 9 | 43.5 | 114 | 232.5 |

It is known that $x$ and $y$ are related by an equation $y = ax^3 - bx$, where $a$ and $b$ are constants.

(a) Change the equation into the linear form.

(b) Find $a$ and $b$.

**4**

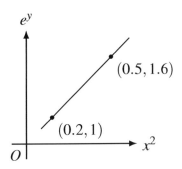

Variables $x$ and $y$ are such that, when $e^y$ is plotted against $x^2$, a straight line graph passing through the points $(0.2, 1)$ and $(0.5, 1.6)$ is obtained.

(a) Find the value of $e^y$ when $x = 0$.

(b) Express $y$ in terms of $x$.

# Answerkey for Practice Problems

**1.**

(a) $y = 1.6x + \dfrac{12}{x}$

(b) $x = \dfrac{330}{4}$

**2.**

(a) $\lg(y) = -\dfrac{1}{3}\lg(x) + 4$

(b) $y = \dfrac{10^4}{\sqrt[3]{x}}$

(c) $x = (\dfrac{100}{7})^3$

**3.**

(a) $\dfrac{y}{x} = ax^2 - b$

(b) $a = 2, b = -4$

**4.**

(a) $e^y = 0.6$

(b) $y = \ln(2x^2 + 0.6)$

# Topic 9

# Functions

- ✓ Essential Knowledge for Functions
- ✓ Quick Facts for Transformation
- ✓ Absolute-valued Function

## 9.1 Essential Knowledge for Functions

Relation is a relation between $x$ and $y$. A function, a special type of relation, sends an input $x$, domain, onto a unique image $y$, range.

$$f : x \longrightarrow y$$

In order to distinguish function from relation, we can use graphs. The graph of a function passes a vertical line test, whereas that of a relation does not. For IGCSE course, the composition of function matters a lot. In other words, functions can be combined. The composition of two functions $y = f(x)$ and $y = g(x)$ results in a new function, where the order matters.

$$(f \circ g)(x) = f(g(x)) \neq g(f(x)) = (g \circ f)(x)$$

Generally, they are not equal. If they are equal, then they are good candidates for inverse function of one another. Same functions can be composed with itself, and $f^2$ is used in IGCSE coursework, which means $f^2 = ff = f(f(x))$. Also, note that the composition order is reversed for inverse functions, i.e.,

$$(f \circ g)^{-1} = g^{-1} \circ f^{-1}$$

In order for a function to have a unique inverse function, it must be one-to one function.

- $y = x^2$: this is two-to-one function.

- $y = \sqrt{x}$ : this is one-to-one function.

There are two criteria to check whether two functions are inverse to one another.

- $f(f^{-1}(x)) = f^{-1}(f(x)) = x$

- The graphs of $y = f(x)$ and $y = f^{-1}(x)$ are reflections of each other in the line $y = x$.

The following two properties are useful when we solve inverse function problems.

1. $f(a) = b \implies a = f^{-1}(b)$.

2. If $f = f^{-1}$, then $f$ is self-inverse. The classical example is $y = -x$.

## Example

List three examples of $f(f(x)) = x$.

**Solution**

$f(x) = -x$, $f(x) = \dfrac{1}{x}$, and $f(x) = x$ are three examples of self-inverse function $y = f(x)$.

---

**1** The function $f$ is defined by $f : x \mapsto 2x^2 - 8x + 5$ for the domain $0 \leq x \leq 5$. Find the range of $f$.

**2** Functions $f$ and $g$ are defined for $x \in \mathbb{R}$ by

$$f : x \mapsto e^x$$
$$g : x \mapsto 2x - 3$$

(a) Solve the equation $fg(x) = 7$.

(b) Express $h = gf$ in terms of $x$ and state its range.

## 9.2 Quick Facts for Transformation

$y = f(x)$ is the equation of the graph of the function. Here is the useful rule to figure out the transformations applied to a function.

- $y = -f(x)$ : a reflection of $y = f(x)$ about the $x$-axis.

- $y = f(-x)$ : a reflection of $y = f(x)$ about the $y$-axis.

- $y = a + f(x)$ : a vertical shift of $y = f(x)$.

- $y = f(x+a)$ : a horizontal shift of $y = f(x)$.

- $y = f(kx)$: a horizontal scaling of $y = f(x)$, changing the width while the height remains unchanged.

- $y = kf(x)$: a vertical scaling of $y = f(x)$, changing the height while the width remains unchanged.

### Example

If $f(3) = 4$, then $f(-x+2) = y$ transforms $(3,4)$ into $(a,b)$. Find the values of $a$ and $b$.

**Solution**

$f(-x+2) = y \implies f(-(x-2)) = y$. Hence, $(3,4) \to (-3,4) \to (-1,4)$. Therefore, $a = -1$ and $b = 4$.

---

**3** The function $g$ is defined by $g : x \longmapsto 2x^2 - 8x + 5$ for domain $x \geq k$.

(a) Find the smallest value os $k$ for which $g$ has an inverse.

(b) For this value of $k$, find an expression for $g^{-1}$.

**4** Functions $f$ and $g$ are defined, for $x \in \mathbb{R}$, by

$$f : x \longmapsto 3x - 7$$
$$g : x \longmapsto \frac{12}{x-2}, x \neq 2$$

(a) Find $f^{-1}$ and $g^{-1}$ in terms of $x$, stating the value of $x$ for which $g^{-1}$ is not defined.

(b) Find the values of $x$ for which $fg(x) = x$.

(c) Sketch the graphs of $f$ and $f^{-1}$ on the same diagram, giving the coordinates of the points of intersection of each graph with the axes.

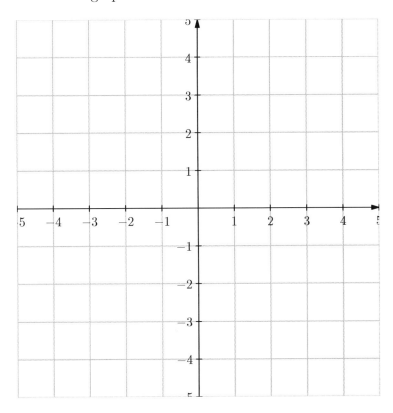

**5** A function defined by $f: x \longmapsto \dfrac{e^x + 1}{4}$ for the domain $x \geq 0$.

(a) Evaluate $f^2(0)$.

(b) Obtain an expression for $f^{-1}$.

(c) State the domain and the range of $f^{-1}$.

## 9.3 Absolute-valued function

Modulus of $x$, or absolute value of $x$, can be written as

$$|x| = \begin{cases} x & \text{for } x \geq 0 \\ -x & \text{for } x < 0 \end{cases}$$

In order to solve an absolute-valued inequality, we use

- $|x| < k \implies -k < x < k$

- $|x| > k \implies x < -k \text{ or } x > k$

In order to draw $y = |f(x)|$, we first draw the graph of $y = f(x)$ and then reflect any negative portion of the graph in the $x$-axis.

**6** Sketch, on the same diagram, the graphs of $y = |x| + 1$ and $y = |2x - 3|$, and state the number of solutions of the equation $|2x - 3| = |x| + 1$.

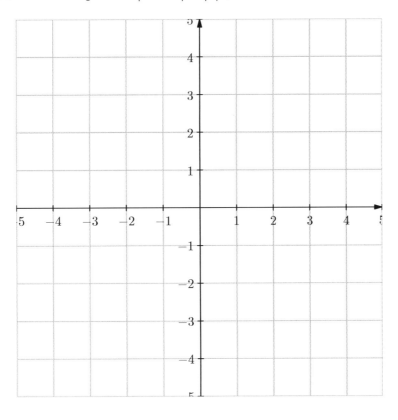

**7** Solve the following questions.

(a) Sketch on the same diagram the graphs of $y = |2x+3|$ and $y = 1-x$.

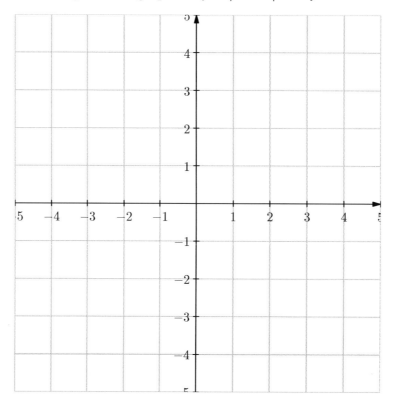

(b) Hence, find the values of $x$ for which $x + |2x+3| = 1$.

**8** Given that each of the following functions is defined for the domain $-2 \leq x \leq 3$, find the range of

(a) $f : x \longmapsto 2 - 3x$

(b) $g : x \longmapsto |2 - 3x|$

(c) $h : x \longmapsto 2 - |3x|$

State which of the functions $f, g$ and $h$ has an inverse.

**9** If the function $g$ is defined by $g : x \longmapsto |x^2 - 8x + 7|$ for the domain $3 \leq x \leq k$, determine the largest value of $k$ for which $g^{-1}$ exists.

# Answerkey for Practice Problems

**1.** $[-3, 15]$

**2.**

(a) $x = \dfrac{\ln 7 + 3}{2}$

(b) $2e^x - 3$, $y > -3$

**3.**

(a) $k = 2$

(b) $y = \dfrac{x+3}{2} + 2$

**4.**

(a) $f^{-1}(x) = \dfrac{x+7}{3}$, $g^{-1}(x) = \dfrac{12}{x} + 2$ for $x \neq 0$.

(b) $x = -10, 5$

(c)

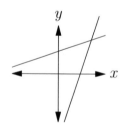

**5.**

(a) $\dfrac{e^{\frac{1}{2}} + 1}{4}$

(b) $\dfrac{e^x}{4} + \dfrac{1}{4}$

(c) Domain is the set of $x$ such that $x \geq \dfrac{1}{2}$, and the range is the set of $y$ such that $y \geq 0$.

**6.**

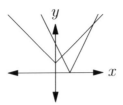

The solutions are $x = \dfrac{4}{3}, 4$

**7.**

(a)

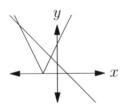

(b) $x = -\dfrac{2}{3}, -4$

**8.**

(a) $[-7, 8]$

(b) $[0, 8]$

(c) $[-7, 2]$

Only (a) has an inverse.

**9.** $k = 4$

# Topic 10

# Trigonometry

- ✓ Trigonometric Ratio
- ✓ Trigonometric Functions
- ✓ Transformation of Trigonometric Functions
- ✓ Other Trigonometric Functions
- ✓ Trigonometric Identities
- ✓ Trigonometric Equations

## 10.1 Trigonometric Ratio

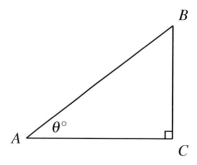

Given a right triangle ABC and an angle $\theta$, there are six trigonometric ratios.

- Sine : the ratio of opposite to hypotenuse, i.e., $\sin\theta = \dfrac{a}{c}$.

- Cosine : the ratio of adjacent to hypotenuse, i.e., $\cos\theta = \dfrac{b}{c}$.

- Tangent : the ratio of opposite to adjacent, i.e., $\tan\theta = \dfrac{a}{b}$.

- Cosecant : the reciprocal of sine, i.e., $\csc\theta = \dfrac{1}{\sin\theta}$.

- Secant : the reciprocal of cosine, i.e., $\sec\theta = \dfrac{1}{\cos\theta}$.

- Cotangent : the reciprocal of tangent, i.e., $\cot\theta = \dfrac{1}{\tan\theta}$.

**1** Fill the blanks.

| $\theta$ | 30° | 45° | 60° |
|---|---|---|---|
| $\sin\theta$ | | | |
| $\cos\theta$ | | | |
| $\tan\theta$ | | | |

Two special triangles, $30° - 60° - 90°$ and $45° - 45° - 90°$, result in trigonometric ratios. Other than tangent values, sine value and cosine value are either $\frac{1}{2}, \frac{\sqrt{2}}{2}$, or $\frac{\sqrt{3}}{2}$. Notice that $\cos(45°)$ or $\sin(45°)$ are $\frac{1}{\sqrt{2}}$. If the denominator is rationalized, then the ratio turns into $\frac{\sqrt{2}}{2}$. Other than special ratios, when one of the trigonometric ratios is given, we can find the other ratio by creating an associated triangle.

**2** If $\tan\theta = 3$, find $\cos\theta$ and $\sin\theta$ for an acute angle $\theta$.

Reference angle is an acute angle formed between the $x$-axis and the rotated ray.

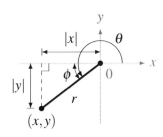

**3** If $0° < \theta < 360°$, and $\theta$ has the reference angle (or base angle) of $45°$, find $\theta$ if it is in

(a) the 2nd quadrant.  (b) the 3rd quadrant.  (c) the 4th quadrant.

**4** Without using a calculator, evaluate

(a) $\dfrac{\cos 45°}{\sin 60° + \cos 30°}$

(b) $\tan 45° - \tan 30° \tan 60°$

(c) $\dfrac{\sin 27°}{\cos 63°}$

**5** Find the reference angle for the given values of $\theta$.

(a) $\theta = 135°$.

(b) $\theta = 450°$.

(c) $\theta = -35°$.

(d) $\theta = -120°$.

**6** Using a right triangle, prove the complementary angle theorem.

$$\sin(90° - \theta) = \cos(\theta)$$
$$\cos(90° - \theta) = \sin(\theta)$$
$$\tan(90° - \theta) = \cot(\theta)$$

**7** If $\sin \theta = \dfrac{1}{2}$, find the value of $\cos(90° - \theta) \sin(\theta)$.

**8** Find $\cos\theta, \sin\theta, \tan\theta$ when $\theta = 225°$.

**9** If $\cos\theta = -\dfrac{2}{3}$ and $180° < \theta < 270°$, find $\tan\theta$ and $\sin\theta$.

## 10.2 Trigonometric Functions

In this section, we will consider $\pi$ as $180°$. This conversion will be covered in detail. Let's first define the terms for two functions.

**Periodic Function**
Graph portions are eternally copy-and-pasted.

**Bounded Function**
Graph has some maximum and minimum.

**(1) Sine Function :** $y = \sin(x)$

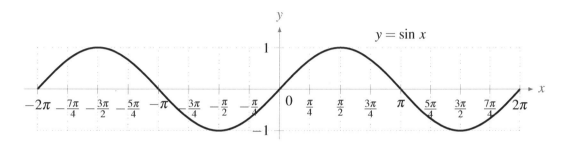

Inputs are the amount of rotation of a ray counter-clockwise, and outputs are $y$-coordinate of the end-tip of a ray on a unit circle. Look at the graph, which is bounded and periodic.

1. Domain(the set of $x$-values) is $\mathbb{R}$.

2. Range(the set of $y$-values) is $[-1, 1]$.

3. Period is $2\pi$.

4. This is an odd function, satisfying $\sin(-x) = -\sin(x)$.

**(2) Cosine Function :** $y = \cos(x)$

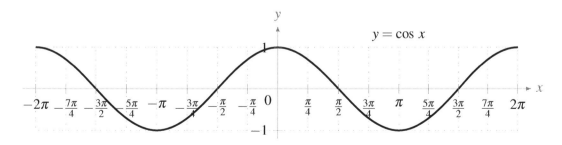

Inputs are the amount of rotation of a ray counter-clockwise, and outputs are the $x$-coordinate of the end-tip of a ray on the unit circle. Like sine graph, the graph is bounded and periodic.

1. Domain(the set of *x*-values) is $\mathbb{R}$.

2. Range(the set of *y*-values) is $[-1, 1]$.

3. Period is $2\pi$.

4. This is an even function, satisfying $\cos(-x) = \cos(x)$.

**(3) Tangent Function :** $y = \tan(x)$

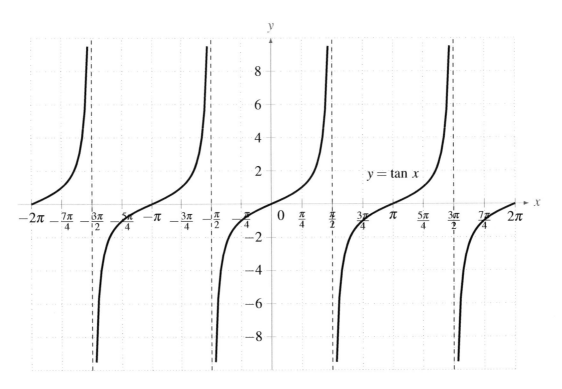

Inputs are the amount of rotation of a ray counter-clockwise, and outputs are the slope of the end-tip of a ray on a unit circle. This function is not bounded, but periodic.

1. Domain is $\mathbb{R} \setminus \{n\pi + \frac{\pi}{2}\}$

2. Range is $\mathbb{R}$.

3. Period is $\pi$.

4. It is an odd function, satisfying $\tan(-x) = -\tan(x)$.

## 10.3 Transformation of Trigonometric Functions

(1) Sinusoidal Function :

$$y = A\sin(B(x-C)) + D \text{ or } y = A\cos(B(x-C)) + D$$

1. Maximum $= |A| + D$

2. Minimum $= -|A| + D$

3. Period $= \dfrac{2\pi}{|B|}$

Let's look at the graph of $y = \sin(2x)$ in the figure below.

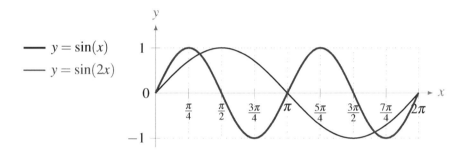

Also, look at the graph of $y = 3\cos(2x)$ below, which changes amplitude and period at the same time.

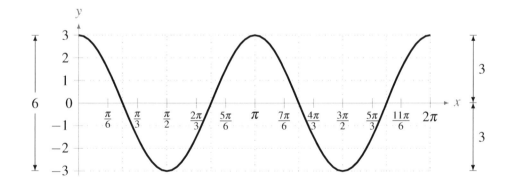

✓ The period is shrunk by a factor of 2, so it must be $\dfrac{2\pi}{2} = \pi$.

✓ The amplitude is vertically stretched by a factor of 3, so it must be 3.

(2) Tangent Function :
$$y = A\tan(B(x-c)) + D$$

where $A$ affects how steep the graph looks like, $B$ affects period, $C$ and $D$ affect translation. Here is the following property of tangent function.

1. Maximum $= \infty$

2. Minimum $= -\infty$

3. Period $= \dfrac{\pi}{|B|}$

**10** If $(\sin\theta + 1)(\cos\theta - 2) = 0$, find the value of $\theta$ for $0° \leq \theta \leq 360°$.

**11** Given $0 \leq x \leq 2\pi$, find the range of values of $3 - 2\cos(x)$.

## 10.4 Other Trigonometric Functions

**(1) Secant Function :** $y = \sec(x)$

Secant function is a reciprocal of cosine function. Mathematical expression for the secant function is

$$f(x) = \sec(x) = \frac{1}{\cos(x)}$$

In this case, domain must be carefully considered. In other words, the values of $x$ such that $\cos(x) = 0$ should be eliminated from our domain because those values make the function undefined.

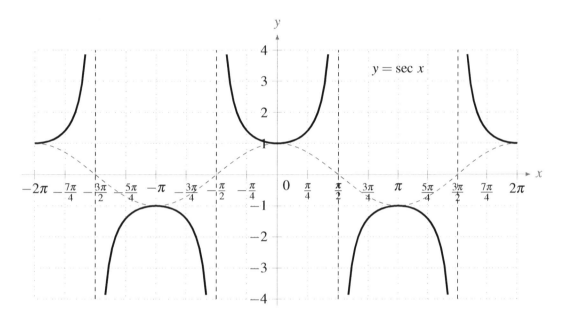

The following properties are satisfied.

1. Domain = the set of all values of $x$ except $x = \pm\frac{\pi}{2}, \pm\frac{3\pi}{2}, \cdots$.

2. Range = the set of all values of $y$ such that $y \leq -1$ or $y \geq 1$.

3. There are infinitely many vertical asymptotes $x = \pm\frac{\pi}{2}, \pm\frac{3\pi}{2}, \cdots$.

4. Period = same as that of cosine.

5. Discontinuous function, which means this is disconnected.

6. This is even function, whose graph is symmetric with respect to $y$-axis.

**(2) Cosecant Function :** $y = \csc(x)$

Cosecant function is a reciprocal of sine function.

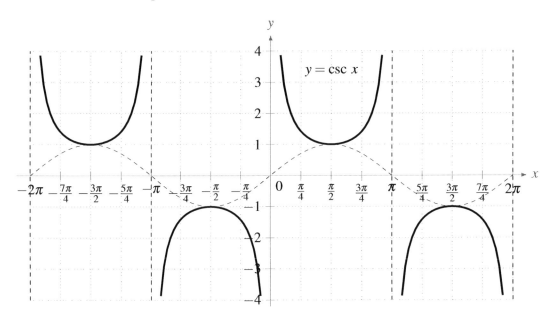

The following properties are satisfied.

1. Domain = the set of all values of $x$ except $x = \pm\pi, \pm 2\pi, \pm 3\pi \cdots$.

2. Range = the set of all values of $y$ such that $y \leq -1$ or $y \geq 1$.

3. There are infinitely many vertical asymptotes $x = 0, \pm\pi, \pm 2\pi, \pm 3\pi, \cdots$.

4. Period = same as that of sine.

5. Discontinuous function, which means this is disconnected.

6. This is odd function, whose graph is symmetric with respect to the origin.

As one can see from the two graphs, the reciprocal function satisfies four major properties in connection with the original function.

✓ The sign of $y$-value does not change. For instance, if the original value is positive, then the reciprocal value is also positive.

✓ Increasing(or decreasing) portion of the original $\iff$ Decreasing(or increasing) portion of the reciprocal.

✓ The $x$-intercept $\iff$ The vertical asymptote.

✓ $y \to \pm\infty \iff y \to 0$.

## (3) Cotangent Function : $y = \cot(x)$

Cotangent function is a reciprocal of tangent function. Mathematical expression for the cotangent function is

$$f(x) = \cot(x) = \frac{1}{\tan(x)}$$

Similar to $\csc(x)$, we do not allow $\sin(x) = 0$ for $x$ values. Hence, the domain for cotangent function is equivalent to the domain for cosecant function. The following lists are the properties of cotangent function.

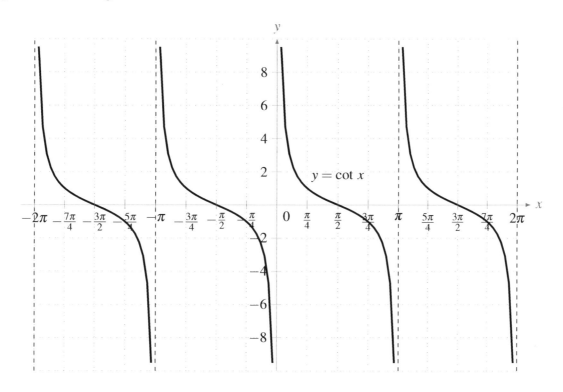

1. Domain = the set of all values of $x$ except $x = \pm\pi, \pm 2\pi, \pm 3\pi \cdots$.

2. Range = $\mathbb{R}$.

3. There are infinitely many vertical asymptotes $x = 0, \pm\pi, \pm 2\pi, \pm 3\pi, \cdots$.

4. Period = same as that of tangent.

5. Discontinuous function, which means this is disconnected.

6. This is odd function, whose graph is symmetric with respect to the origin.

**12** Solve $\sec(-x) = 2$ for $0 < x < 2\pi$.

**13** If an angle $A$ is obtuse and $\cot(A) = -2$, find the value of

(a) $\sec(A)$

(b) $\csc(A)$

## 10.5 Trigonometric Identities

The followings are important important formulas with respect to trigonometric expressions. Memorize them by heart.

> **Trigonometric Identities**
>
> - $\cos(-x) = \cos(x)$, $\sin(-x) = -\sin(x)$, and $\tan(-x) = -\tan(x)$.
> - $\cos^2(x) + \sin^2(x) = 1$, $\tan^2(x) + 1 = \sec^2(x)$, and $\cot^2(x) + 1 = \csc^2(x)$.
> - $\cos(x \pm y) = \cos(x)\cos(y) \mp \sin(x)\sin(y)$
> - $\sin(x \pm y) = \sin(x)\cos(y) \pm \cos(x)\sin(y)$
> - $\cos(\frac{\pi}{2} - x) = \sin(x)$ or vice versa.

**14** Prove that $\dfrac{1}{1 - \cos\theta} + \dfrac{1}{1 + \cos\theta} = 2\csc^2\theta$.

**15** Prove that $\dfrac{1}{1 - \sin(x)} - \dfrac{1}{1 + \sin(x)} = 2\tan(x)\sec(x)$.

**16** Given an acute angle $\sin(x) = p$, find an expression, in terms of $p$, for $\csc(2x)$.

**17** Prove that $\dfrac{1}{\tan\theta + \cot\theta} = \sin\theta\cos\theta$.

**18** Show that $(1+\sec\theta)(1-\cos\theta) = \sin\theta\tan\theta$.

**19** Show $\sin^2(x) = \dfrac{1-\cos(2x)}{2}$.

**20** Prove $(1+\tan(x))^2 + (1-\tan(x))^2 = 2\sec^2(x)$.

**21** Prove that $(1+\sec\theta)(\csc\theta - \cot\theta) = \tan\theta$.

## 10.6 Trigonometric Equations

### Solving Trigonometric Equations

Solving trigonometric equations usually simulate the following steps, using some knowledge about sine, cosine, and tangent properties. Here is the general rule for solving trigonometric equations.

1. Find the reference angle.

2. Remember that $\sin(\theta)$ is the $y$-coordinate, $\cos(\theta)$ is the $x$-coordinate and $\tan(\theta)$ is the gradient.

3. Find the correct values that fit in the range of $x$-values.

**22** Solve $\cos(2x) = \sin(2x)$ for $0° \leq x \leq 360°$.

**23** Solve $\cot^2(x) + 3\csc(x) = 3$ for $0° \leq x \leq 360°$.

**24** Solve $\sin(x+\frac{\pi}{4}) = -\frac{1}{2}$ for $0 \leq x \leq 2\pi$ radians, giving each answer as a multiple of $\pi$.

**25** Solve $2\cos(x)\cot(x) + 1 = \cot(x) + 2\cos(x)$ for $0 < x < \pi$.

# 10.7 Law of Sines and Law of Cosines

## (1) The First Law of Sines

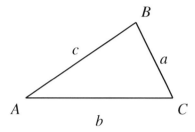

Given the lengths of two sides of a triangle and the size of the included angle, the area of triangle is defined by

$$\begin{aligned}\text{Area} &= \frac{1}{2}ab\sin(\angle C) \\ &= \frac{1}{2}bc\sin(\angle A) \\ &= \frac{1}{2}ac\sin(\angle B)\end{aligned}$$

## (2) The Second Law of Sines

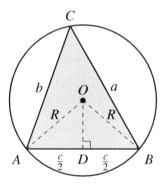

There is an invariant ratio for a triangle such that

$$\frac{a}{\sin A} = \frac{b}{\sin B} = \frac{c}{\sin C} = 2R$$

where the rule is used in the cases for

1. two angles and one side
2. two sides and non-included angle

The law of sine can be easily deduced using the property of circumcenter, the point of concurrency for perpendicular bisectors.

## (3) The Law of Cosine

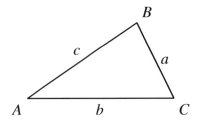

Given the measure of three side lengths, we have the formula

$$a^2 = b^2 + c^2 - 2bc\cos(A)$$
$$b^2 = a^2 + c^2 - 2ac\cos(B)$$
$$c^2 = a^2 + b^2 - 2ab\cos(C)$$

The law of cosines is used when we have to figure out side lengths or angles with

1. three side lengths

2. two side lengths and one common angle

**26** What is the cosine of the largest interior angle of a triangle with 4, 5 and 6?

## (4) Heron's Formula

Heron's formula is useful to find the area of triangle when the side-lengths are all given.

$$A = \sqrt{p(p-a)(p-b)(p-c)}$$

where $p = \dfrac{a+b+c}{2}$. Heron's formula can be directly deduced by the law of cosine and the law of sine. The deduction of Heron's formula requires bits of algebra.

$$\begin{aligned}
\text{Area of } \triangle ABC &= \frac{ab}{2}\sin(\theta) \\
&= \frac{1}{2}ab\sqrt{1-\cos^2(\theta)} \\
&= \frac{1}{2}ab\sqrt{1-\frac{(c^2-a^2-b^2)^2}{4a^2b^2}} \\
&= \sqrt{\frac{4a^2b^2-(c^2-a^2-b^2)^2}{16}} \\
&= \sqrt{\frac{(2ab-c^2+a^2+b^2)(2ab+c^2-a^2-b^2)}{16}} \\
&= \sqrt{\frac{((a+b)^2-c^2)(c^2-(a-b)^2)}{16}} \\
&= \sqrt{\frac{(a+b+c)(-a+b+c)(a-b+c)(a+b-c)}{16}} \\
&= \sqrt{p(p-a)(p-b)(p-c)}
\end{aligned}$$

**27** Find the area of a triangle with side lengths of 4, 5, and 6.

**28** The diagram illustrates a circle with center $O$ and radius $r$ cm. Find, in terms of $r$ and $\theta$, an expression for the length of the chord $AB$.

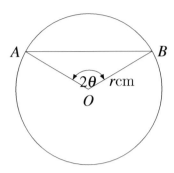

# Answerkey for Practice Problems

**1.**

$\sin(30°) = \dfrac{1}{2}, \sin(45°) = \dfrac{\sqrt{2}}{2}, \sin(60°) = \dfrac{\sqrt{3}}{2}$

$\cos(30°) = \dfrac{\sqrt{3}}{2}, \cos(45°) = \dfrac{\sqrt{2}}{2}, \cos(60°) = \dfrac{1}{2}$

$\tan(30°) = \dfrac{1}{\sqrt{3}}, \tan(45°) = 1, \tan(60°) = \sqrt{3}$

**2.** $\cos\theta = \dfrac{1}{\sqrt{10}}, \sin\theta = \dfrac{3}{\sqrt{10}}$

**3.**

(a) 135°

(b) 225°

(c) 315°

**4.**

(a) $\dfrac{\sqrt{6}}{6}$

(b) 0

(c) 1

**5.**

(a) 45°

(b) 90°

(c) 35°

(d) 60°

**6.**

Given a right triangle, $\theta$ and $90° - \theta$ are complementary. Then, $\sin(\theta) = \dfrac{\text{Opp}}{\text{Hyp}}$ whereas $\cos(90° - \theta) = \dfrac{\text{Opp}}{\text{Hyp}}$. Similarly, $\cos(\theta) = \dfrac{\text{Adj}}{\text{Hyp}}$ whereas $\sin(\theta) = \dfrac{\text{Adj}}{\text{Hyp}}$. Hence, $\tan(90° - \theta) = \dfrac{\cos(\theta)}{\sin(\theta)} = \cot(\theta)$.

**7.** $\dfrac{1}{4}$

**8.** $\cos(225°) = -\dfrac{1}{\sqrt{2}}, \sin(225°) = -\dfrac{1}{\sqrt{2}}, \tan(225°) = 1$

**9.** $\tan\theta = \dfrac{\sqrt{5}}{2}, \sin\theta = -\dfrac{\sqrt{5}}{3}$

**10.** $\theta = 270°$

**11.** $[1, 5]$

**12.** $\dfrac{\pi}{3}, \dfrac{5\pi}{3}$

**13.** (a) $-\sqrt{5}$ \hspace{2cm} (b) $\dfrac{\sqrt{5}}{2}$

**14.**

$$\dfrac{1}{1-\cos(\theta)} + \dfrac{1}{1+\cos(\theta)} = \dfrac{2}{1-\cos^2(\theta)}$$
$$= \dfrac{2}{\sin^2(\theta)}$$
$$= 2\csc^2(\theta).$$

**15.**

$$\dfrac{1}{1-\sin(x)} - \dfrac{1}{1+\sin(x)} = \dfrac{2\sin(x)}{1-\sin^2(x)}$$
$$= \dfrac{2\sin(x)}{\cos^2(x)}$$
$$= 2\dfrac{\sin(x)}{\cos(x)}\dfrac{1}{\cos(x)}$$
$$= 2\tan(x)\sec(x)$$

16. $\dfrac{1}{2p\sqrt{1-p^2}}$

17.
$$\begin{aligned}\dfrac{1}{\tan(\theta)+\cot(\theta)} &= \dfrac{\sin(\theta)\cos(\theta)}{\sin^2(\theta)+\cos^2(\theta)} \\ &= \dfrac{\sin(\theta)\cos(\theta)}{1} \\ &= \sin(\theta)\cos(\theta)\end{aligned}$$

18.
$$\begin{aligned}(1+\sec(\theta))(1-\cos(\theta)) &= 1-\cos(\theta)+\sec(\theta)-1 \\ &= -\cos(\theta)+\dfrac{1}{\cos(\theta)} \\ &= \dfrac{-\cos^2(\theta)}{\cos(\theta)}+\dfrac{1}{\cos(\theta)} \\ &= \dfrac{1-\cos^2(\theta)}{\cos(\theta)} \\ &= \dfrac{\sin^2(\theta)}{\cos(\theta)} \\ &= \sin(\theta)\dfrac{\sin(\theta)}{\cos(\theta)} \\ &= \sin(\theta)\tan(\theta)\end{aligned}$$

19.
$$\begin{aligned}\dfrac{1-\cos(2x)}{2} &= \dfrac{1-(\cos^2(\theta)-\sin^2(\theta))}{2} \\ &= \dfrac{(1-\cos^2(\theta))+\sin^2(\theta)}{2} \\ &= \dfrac{2\sin^2(\theta)}{2} \\ &= \sin^2(\theta)\end{aligned}$$

**20.**

$$(1+\tan(x))^2 + (1-\tan(x))^2 = 1 + 2\tan(x) + \tan^2(x) + 1 - 2\tan(x) + \tan^2(x)$$
$$= 2 + 2\tan^2(x)$$
$$= 2(1+\tan^2(x))$$
$$= 2\sec^2(x)$$

**21.**

$$(1+\sec(\theta))(\csc(\theta) - \cot(\theta)) = \frac{1+\cos(\theta)}{\cos(\theta)} \frac{1-\cos(\theta)}{\sin(\theta)}$$
$$= \frac{1-\cos^2(\theta)}{\cos(\theta)\sin(\theta)}$$
$$= \frac{\sin^2(\theta)}{\cos(\theta)\sin(\theta)}$$
$$= \frac{\sin(\theta)}{\cos(\theta)}$$
$$= \tan(\theta)$$

**22.** $x = 22.5°, 112.5°, 202.5°, 292.5°$

**23.** $x = 14.4775°, 165.522°$

**24.** $\dfrac{7\pi}{6}, \dfrac{11\pi}{6}$

**25.** $\dfrac{\pi}{4}, \dfrac{\pi}{3}$

**26.** $\cos(\theta) = \dfrac{1}{8}$.

**27.** The area equals $\sqrt{7.5(7.5-4)(7.5-5)(7.5-6)} \approx 5.728$.

**28.** $AB = \sqrt{2r^2(1-\cos(2\theta))}$

# Topic 11

# Counting and Binomial Theorem

- ✓ Counting Principle
- ✓ Permutation and Combination
- ✓ The Binomial Expansion

## 11.1 Counting Principle

If there are *m* different ways of performing an operation and for each of these there are *n* different ways of performing a second **independent** operation, then there are *mn* different ways of performing the two operations in succession. The word **and** suggests multiplying the given possibilities. The word **or** suggests adding the possibilities.

First, for $n \geq 1$, $n!$ is the product of the first $n$ positive integers such that

$$n! = n(n-1)(n-2)\cdots \times 2 \times 1$$

Second, the rules of addition and multiplication can be catorized by the following information.

> **Rules of Addition and Multiplication**
>
> 1. Add when the method of computation is different, i.e., difficult to simplify the calculation by multiplication. For instance, if we have to count the number of multiples of 2 or 3, we cannot count the numbers separately and add the results.
>
> 2. Add when each case has different condition to satisfy, i.e., easy to enumerate in cases. For instance, if there are four digit numbers where the last digit is a multiple of 3. Then, we case-enumerate.
>
> 3. Multiply when the method of computation is equal, i.e., easy to simplify the calculation. For instance, if the counts are repetitive, we multiply.
>
> 4. Multiply when all cases that occur consecutively satisfy the given condition. For instance, if you arrange objects in order, then you count with "first, second, third, and so on". In this case, we separately count the numbers in each step, then multiply the results.

Remember that we use the two principles, according to the following rules.

- multiply if ongoing actions are incomplete.
- add if we count with casework.

Caseworks must be exhaustive and disjoint. If there is any overlapping count, we should get rid of the overcounts by subtracting or dividing the counts.

**1** If two different dice are thrown, find the total number of cases when the sum of the face values is a multiple of 4.

**2** If an event $A$ has three cases, and event $B$ two cases, find the number of ways that event $A$ and $B$ occur consecutively.

## 11.2 Permutation and Combination

Out of *n* distinct objects, the number of arrangements for *r* different objects is called the permutation of *r* objects out of *n* different objects, which is defined by

$$P_r^n = {}_nP_r = \frac{n!}{(n-r)!}$$

Factorial is the permutation of *n* objects out of *n* objects, which is symbolized by

$$n! = n \times (n-1) \times (n-2) \cdots 3 \times 2 \times 1$$

On the other hand, the number of selections of *r* different objects out of *n* objects is called the combination, which is defined by

$$C_r^n = {}_nC_r = \binom{n}{r} = \frac{{}_nP_r}{r!}$$

Here, dividing by *n*! means that *n*! number of choices is considered to be 1.

**3** A chess association runs a tournament with 16 teams. In how many different ways could the top 8 positions be filled on the competition ladder?

**4** How many different teams of 4 can be selected from a squad of 7 if:

(a) there are no restrictions

(b) the teams must include a specific captain?

> **Example**
> How many distinct arrangements are there for "IRONMAN"?
>
> **Solution**
> Since there are two $N$'s repeated, the total number of arrangements is $\dfrac{7!}{2!}$.

**5** How many letter arrangements are possible for a word

(a) COUNT? (b) CONNECTIONS?

**6** If there are 2 boys and 5 girls, how many ways are there to arrange students in order such that

(a) 2 boys are adjacent to one another?

(b) 2 boys are not adjacent to one another?

**7** Suppose there are 10 classes. If three water filter, not distinguishable from one another, were to be installed so that no two classes that have water filter installed are adjacent to each other, how many ways are there to pick those three classes to install the filter?

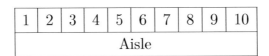

> **Example**
>
> Assume there are five people in a row. If Bob and Charles must be adjacent to one another, how many different arrangements of people can be made?
>
> > Put Bob and Charles in one magical bundle. Then, arrange four people (three others and one magical bundle). Since there are two possible arrangements for Bob and Charles to be placed inside the magical bundle, the total possibilities are $4! \times 2! = 48$.

**8** If there are 3 comic books, 5 classics, and 3 novels, how many ways are there to arrange all the books in a shelf in order such that no comic book is adjacent to one another?

## 11.3 The Binomial Expansion

The sum $a+b$ is called a binomial, since it contains two terms. Any expression of the form $(a+b)^n$ is called **a power of a binomial**. After observing some patterns for $n$, we can conclude that

$$(a+b)^n = a^n + \binom{n}{1}a^{n-1}b + \cdots + \binom{n}{r}a^{n-r}b^r + \cdots + b^n$$

where $\binom{n}{r}$ is the binomial coefficient of $a^{n-r}b^r$ for $r = 0, 1, \cdots, n$. The general term or $(r+1)$th term in the binomial expansion is $T_{r+1} = \binom{n}{r}a^{n-r}b^r$. The sigma notation produces the following formula

$$(a+b)^n = \sum_{r=0}^{n} a^{n-r}b^r$$

> **Example**
>
> Find the 3rd row of Pascal's triangle.
>
> The first row is 1. The second row is also 1,1. Hence, the third row must be 1,2,1. The fourth row, in addition is 1,3,3,1.

**9** Find the 5th row of Pascal's triangle.

**10** Expand $(2x+3y)^4$.

**11** Expand $(x-2y)^5$.

**12** Given $(x-2y)^5$, find the third term in an ascending order of $x$.

**13** Find the term independent of $x$ in the expansion of $(x^2 - \frac{2}{x})^6$.

# Answerkey for Practice Problems

1. 9

2. 6

3. $_{16}P_8$

4. 
   
   (a) $_7C_4$
   
   (b) $_6C_3$

5. 
   
   (a) $5!$
   
   (b) $\dfrac{11!}{2!2!3!}$

6. 
   
   (a) $6! \times 2!$
   
   (b) $5 \cdot 6!$

7. 56

8. $_8P_8 \times {_9P_3}$

9. $1, 4, 6, 4, 1$

10. $16x^4 + 96x^3y + 216x^2y^2 + 216xy^3 + 81y^4$

11. $x^5 - 10x^4y + 40x^3y^2 - 80x^2y^3 + 80xy^4 - 32y^5$

12. $-80x^2y^3$

13. 240

# Topic 12

# Differentiation

- ✓ Instantaneous Rate of Change
- ✓ Basic Derivatives
- ✓ Differentiation Rules
- ✓ Tangent and Normal Lines

## 12.1 Instantaneous Rate of Change

Given a function $y = f(x)$, the instantaneous rate of change of $f(x)$ at $x = a$ is found by

$$\lim_{x \to a} \frac{f(x) - f(a)}{x - a}$$

Generally, given a function $y = f(x)$, the first derivative of $f(x)$ is given by

$$\lim_{h \to 0} \frac{f(x+h) - f(x)}{h}$$

Usually, the derivative of $f(x)$ is written as $f'(x)$ or $\frac{d}{dx} f(x)$. The following properties are satisfied for two differentiable functions $f(x)$ and $g(x)$.

1. $(f(x) \pm g(x))' = f'(x) \pm g'(x)$.

2. $(kf(x))' = kf'(x)$ where $k$ is a constant

### Example
Find the instantaneous rate of change of $y = x^2$ at $x = 1$.

**Solution**
$$f'(1) = \lim_{h \to 0} \frac{(1+h)^2 - 1^2}{h} = \lim_{h \to 0} \frac{1 + 2h + h^2 - 1}{h} = 2.$$

**1** Find the instantaneous rate of change of $f(x) = x^2 + 1$ at $x = 2$, using two definitions.

## 12.2 Basic derivatives

The following lists are the basic derivatives used in IGCSE course.

1. $\dfrac{d}{dx} x^n = n x^{n-1}$

2. $\dfrac{d}{dx} \sin(x) = \cos(x)$

3. $\dfrac{d}{dx} \cos(x) = -\sin(x)$

4. $\dfrac{d}{dx} e^x = e^x$

5. $\dfrac{d}{dx} \ln(x) = \dfrac{1}{x}$

The power rule can be applied to rational $n$. For instance, if $\sqrt{x}$ is given, notice that $\sqrt{x} = x^{\frac{1}{2}}$. The derivative of this is given by $\dfrac{1}{2} x^{-\frac{1}{2}}$ which is neatly written as $\dfrac{1}{2\sqrt{x}}$.

**2** Find $\dfrac{d}{dx}(4x^2 - 3x + 7)$.

**3** Find $\dfrac{d}{dx}(\sqrt{x}+\sin(x))$.

**4** Find $\dfrac{d}{dx}(e^x - \dfrac{3}{x} + \ln(x))$.

## 12.3 Differentiation Rules

- Product rule : $(uv)' = u'v + uv'$ for a shortcut

    The formal version of product rule can be written as

    $$\frac{d}{dx}(f(x)g(x)) = (\frac{d}{dx}f(x))g(x) + f(x)(\frac{d}{dx}g(x))$$

- Quotient rule : $(\frac{u}{v})' = \frac{u'v - uv'}{v^2}$ for a shortcut

    The formal version of product rule can be written as

    $$\frac{d}{dx}(\frac{f(x)}{g(x)}) = \frac{(\frac{d}{dx}f(x))g(x) - f(x)(\frac{d}{dx}g(x))}{(g(x)^2)}$$

- Chain rule : $(f(g(x)))' = f'(g(x))g'(x)$

The chain rule in IGCSE is given by a rule to memorize. In IB, this is not something you memorize but something more natural to do it by hand.

- $\frac{d}{dx}(ax+b)^n = a \cdot n(ax+b)^{n-1}$

- $\frac{d}{dx}\sin(ax+b) = a \cdot \cos(x)$

- $\frac{d}{dx}\cos(ax+b) = a \cdot -\sin(x)$

- $\frac{d}{dx}e^{ax+b} = a \cdot e^{ax+b}$

- $\frac{d}{dx}\ln(ax+b) = \frac{1}{ax+b} \cdot a$

### Example
Find the derivative of $(2x+1)\sin(2x)$.

#### Solution
Since $(uv)' = u'v + uv'$, $((2x+1)\sin(2x))' = 2\sin(2x) + (2x+1)(2\cos(2x))$.

**5** Find $\dfrac{d}{dx}((3x+1)(2x^2+1))$.

**6** Find $\dfrac{d}{dx}(\tan(x))$.

**7** Find $\dfrac{d}{dx}(\sin(3x+1))$.

## 12.4 Tangent and Normal Lines

Given a differentiable function $y = f(x)$, there is a tangent line at $x = a$ satisfying

$$y = f'(a)(x-a) + f(a)$$

Similarly, the normal line at $x = a$ is $y = -\dfrac{1}{f'(a)}(x-a) + f(a)$. The only difference between the tangent line and normal line at $x = a$ is that the slopes are negative reciprocals of each other.

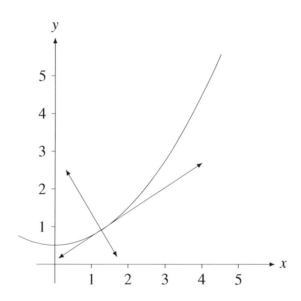

### Example

Find the tangent line and normal line to $y = x^2$ at $x = 1$.

**Solution**

- $y' = 2x$, so $y'(1) = 2$. Hence, the slope of the normal line is $-\dfrac{1}{2}$.

- It passes through $(1, 1^2) = (1, 1)$.

Thus,

1. The tangent line is $y = 2(x-1) + 1 = 2x - 2 + 1 = 2x - 1$.

2. The normal line is $y = -\dfrac{1}{2}(x-1) + 1 = -\dfrac{1}{2}x + \dfrac{1}{2} + 1 = -\dfrac{1}{2}x + \dfrac{3}{2}$.

**8** Find the tangent line equation to the curve $y = \dfrac{4}{x^2} + 1$ at the point where $x = a$. This tangent meets the axes at $P(b,0)$ and $Q(0,b)$. Find the value of $a$ and $b$.

**9** Find the equation of the tangent line to the curve $y = x + x^2$ at the point where $x = a$. Find the values of $a$ for which this line passes through the point $P(2,-3)$. Hence, find the equations of the tangents from $P$ to the curve.

> **Example**
>
> If the tangent line to $y = x^2 + 3x + 2$ has the slope value of 5, find the coordinates of the point of intersection between the tangent line and the curve.
>
> Since $y' = 2x + 3 = 5$, the tangent line has the slope of 5 at $x = 1$. Therefore, $y = 1^2 + 3(1) + 2 = 6$. Thus, the point of intersection must be $(1, 6)$.

**10** Find the coordinates of the two points on the curve $y = 4 - x^2$ whose tangents pass through the point $(-1, 7)$.

# Answerkey for Practice Problems

1. 4

2. $8x - 3$

3. $\dfrac{1}{2\sqrt{x}} + \cos(x)$

4. $e^x + \dfrac{3}{x^2} + \dfrac{1}{x}$

5. $18x^2 + 4x + 3$

6. $\sec^2 x$

7. $3\cos(3x+1)$

8. $a = 2, b = 4$

9. $a = -1, 5,\ y = -x - 1$

10. $(1,3), (-3,-5)$

# Topic 13

# Related Rates

- ✓ Rates of Change
- ✓ Related Rates
- ✓ Small Changes

## 13.1 Rates of Change

The rate of change of a variable $x$ with respect to $t$, time parameter, is given by $\dfrac{dx}{dt}$. Its meaning can be divided into two parts.

> 1. $\dfrac{dx}{dt} > 0$ means $x$ increases as $t$ increases. In other words, $x$ is moving right as $t$ increases.
>
> 2. $\dfrac{dx}{dt} < 0$ means $x$ decreases as $t$ increases. In other words, $x$ is moving left as $t$ increases.

If $\dfrac{dx}{dt} = k$ for some constant $k$, then $x(t) = kt + c$. This type of relation is called the constant rate of change.

**1** The volume, $V$ cm$^3$, of a cube at time $t$ seconds is given by $V = (4 + \dfrac{1}{3}t)^3$. Find the rate at which its volume is increasing at the instant when $t = 2$.

## 13.2 Related Rates

Given an area of circle, $A = \pi r^2$, and the rate of change in radius is given by $r = r(t)$, then the rate at which the area changes with respect to time is given by

$$\frac{dA}{dt} = \frac{dA}{dr}\frac{dr}{dt} = (2\pi r(t)) \cdot \frac{d}{dt}(r(t))$$

which is an application of chain rule.

**2** The surface area of a cube is increasing at $0.2 cm^2 s^{-1}$. Find the rate of increase of the volume when the length of a side is $1cm$.

**3** The radius of a sphere increases at a rate of $2 cm s^{-1}$. Find the rate of increase of its volume when the radius is $3cm$.

**4** A man 1.5m tall is walking at a speed of $2ms^{-1}$ away from a lamppost which has a lamp $5m$ above the ground. Find the rate at which the length of his shadow is increasing. Hence, find the speed of the top of this shadow.

**5** The ladder $AB$ of length $5m$ has one end $A$ leaning against a vertical wall. The other end $B$ rests on the horizontal ground. When $A$ is at a height of $4m$, it slides down the wall at the rate of $2ms^{-1}$. How fast is the other end $B$, sliding along the horizontal ground?

## 13.3 Small Changes

This section, which might be natural if we learn a limit process in detail, is better explained as a formula.

$$\frac{dy}{dx} \approx \frac{\triangle y}{\triangle x}$$

Note that some textbooks use the notation $\delta y$ instead of $\triangle y$. Rearranging this equation results in

$$\triangle y \approx \frac{dy}{dx} \triangle x$$

There are two types of questions for small changes. One asks for approximate change, which is $\triangle y$, and the other asks for approximate value, which is $y$-value.

### Example
Find the approximate value of $\sqrt[3]{7.99}$.

Let $y = \sqrt[3]{x}$. Then, $y' = \dfrac{1}{3\sqrt[3]{x^2}}$.

$$\frac{\sqrt[3]{7.99} - \sqrt[3]{8}}{7.99 - 8} \approx \frac{1}{3\sqrt[3]{4}}$$

$$\sqrt[3]{7.99} - 2 \approx \frac{1}{3\sqrt[3]{4}}(-0.01)$$

$$\sqrt[3]{7.99} \approx 2 - \frac{1}{300\sqrt[3]{4}}$$

**6** Find the approximate change in $y$ if $x$ increases from 2 to 2.02 for $y = x^3$.

### Example

If $y = x^2$, find the approximate value of $\sqrt{9.01}$.

**Solution**

Since $y' = 2x$. Then, by the analysis of small changes,

$$\frac{\sqrt{9.01} - \sqrt{9}}{9.01 - 9} \approx 2(9)$$

$$\sqrt{9.01} - 3 \approx 18(0.01)$$

$$\sqrt{9.01} \approx 3 + 0.18$$

$$\sqrt{9.01} \approx 3.18$$

**7** Given that $y = \sqrt{x}$, find the approximate value for $\sqrt{4.01}$.

# Answerkey for Practice Problems

1. $\dfrac{196}{3}$

2. $\dfrac{1}{20}$

3. $72\pi$

4. $\dfrac{6}{7}$

5. $\dfrac{8}{3}$

6. $12 \times 0.02$

7. $2 + \dfrac{1}{400}$

# Topic 14

# Higher-Derivatives

✓ Meaning of First Derivative

✓ Meaning of Second Derivative

## 14.1 Meaning of First Derivative

Given a differentiable function $y = f(x)$, the meaning of $f'(x)$ can be classified into three cases.

1. $f'(x) = 0$ : such $x$ value is called a critical point. This is called a stationary point. This is when the tangent line is horizontal.

2. $f'(x) > 0$ : $f(x)$ is increasing at $x$.

3. $f'(x) < 0$ : $f(x)$ is decreasing at $x$.

The sign of $f'(x)$ determines whether $f(x)$ has a local maximum(relative maximum) or a local minimum. Here is the first derivative test.

### First Derivative Test

1. local maximum : $f'(x) = 0$ and the sign of $f'(x)$ changes from positive to negative. In other words, $f(x)$ changes from increasing to decreasing.

2. local minimum : $f'(x) = 0$ and the sign of $f'(x)$ changes from negative to positive. In other words, $f(x)$ changes from decreasing to increasing.

3. neither maximum nor minimum : $f'(x) = 0$ and the sign of $f'(x)$ does not change.

A stationary point (critical point) is called a turning point if it is relative maximum or minimum.

**1** Find the relative maximum or minimum values of the curve $y = x^3 - 6x^2 + 9x + 2$.

The Essential Guide to IGCSE: Additional Math

> **Example**
>
> Determine whether the critical point of $y = |x|$ is local minimum, maximum, or neither.
>
> Since $y'$ is undefined at $x = 0$. This is the critical point. Since $y' = -1$ at $x < 0$ and $y' = 1$ at $x > 0$. The function $y = |x|$ has the local minimum value at $x = 0$.

**2** Determine whether $y = x^3 + x - 2$ is an increasing function.

**3** Find and classify the stationary points of the curve $y = x^3 - 3x$, and sketch the curve.

## 14.2 Meaning of Second Derivative

Given a twice-differentiable function $y = f(x)$, the meaning of $f''(x)$ can be classified into three cases.

1. $f''(x) = 0$ : a candidate for inflection point, where the graph of $f(x)$ changes its concavity.

2. $f''(x) > 0$ : $f(x)$ is concave up at $x$.

3. $f''(x) < 0$ : $f(x)$ is concave down at $x$.

Similar to the first derivative, the sign of $f''(x)$ determines whether $f(x)$ has an inflection point. This is how we determine whether $f(x)$ has an inflection point by analyzing the sign of $f''(x)$.

### Second Derivative Test

1. inflection point : $f''(x) = 0$ and the sign of $f''(x)$ changes from positive to negative (or vice versa).

2. not inflection point: $f''(x) = 0$ and the sign of $f''(x)$ does not change.

3. local maximum : $f'(x) = 0$ and $f''(x) < 0$

4. local minimum : $f'(x) = 0$ and $f''(x) > 0$

**4** Two positive quantities $x$ and $y$ vary in such a way that $x^2 y = 9$. Another quantity is defined by $z = 16x + 3y$. Find the values of $x$ and $y$ that make $z$ a minimum.

**5** A piece of wire of length $x$ cm is bent to form a rectangle. Show that the area of the rectangle is maximum when it is a square.

**6** Which point on the curve $y = x^2$ is nearest to the point $(3, 0)$?

# Answerkey for Practice Problems

**1.** $x = 1$ (relative maximum), $x = 3$ (relative minimum)

**2.** Yes, it is increasing for all $x$.

**3.** Stationary points are $x = -1, 1$. The curve has its relative maximum at $x = -1$ and its relative minimum at $x = 1$.

**4.** $x = \dfrac{2}{3}, y = \dfrac{1}{4}$.

**5.** Let $2a + 2b = x$. Then, $f(b) = ab = (\dfrac{x}{2} - b)b$ has its critical point at $b = \dfrac{x}{4}$ because $f'(b) = \dfrac{x}{2} - 2b$. If $b < \dfrac{x}{4}$, then $\dfrac{x}{2} - 2b > 0$. If $b > \dfrac{x}{4}$, then $\dfrac{x}{2} - 2b < 0$. Hence, $b = a = \dfrac{x}{4}$ implies that the area is maximum when it is square.

**6.** $(1, 1)$

# Topic 15

# Integration

- ✓ Indefinite Integral
- ✓ Definite Integral

## 15.1 Indefinite Integral

This is simply the reverse process of differentiation. The most important discovery for Calculus is that integration and differentiation is the reverse process of one another, which is known as the fundamental theorem of calculus.

**Fundamental Theorem of Calculus**

$$\frac{d}{dx}F(x) = f(x)$$

$$\int f(x)dx = F(x) + c$$

**Example**

If $f'(x) = 2x - 3$, where $f(x) = x^2 - 3x$, find $\int f'(x)dx$.

**Solution**

Since $\int f'(x)dx = f(x) + C$, then $\int f'(x)dx = x^2 - 3x + C$.

**1** Given that $y = x\sqrt{2x+15}$, show that $\dfrac{dy}{dx} = \dfrac{k(x+5)}{\sqrt{2x+15}}$, where $k$ is a constant to be found. Hence find $\int \dfrac{x+5}{\sqrt{2x+15}}dx$.

## Properties of Integral

Suppose two functions are integrable. What does it mean to be integrable? Just consider that any function can be integrated if it is continuous. This is not entirely truthful, but it does not hurt us in IGCSE course. Given two integrable functions $f(x)$ and $g(x)$, then

- $\int kf(x)dx = k\int f(x)dx$
- $\int f(x) \pm g(x)dx = \int f(x)dx \pm \int g(x)dx$

The following lists of integrals are used in Additional Math. Good thing about IGCSE test is that the questions give you enough hints to figure out the integral. The lists below are commonly used integral directly derived from differentiation. Other techniques of integration will be extensively covered in IB Math HL/SL courses.

1. $\int x^n dx = \dfrac{x^{n+1}}{n+1} + C$

2. $\int \sin(x)dx = -\cos(x) + C$

3. $\int \cos(x)dx = \sin(x) + C$

4. $\int \sec^2(x)dx = \tan(x) + C$

5. $\int e^x dx = e^x + C$

## U-Substitution

In IGCSE Additional Math, this is not directly considered as an integration technique. Nevertheless, it seems pointless to memorize this as a formula. So, here we deduce the u-substitution technique.

$$\int f(x)dx = \int f(u)du$$

**2** Find $\int \dfrac{10}{(3x-1)^4} dx$.

**3** Solve the following questions.

(a) Given that $y = x\sin(4x)$, find $\dfrac{dy}{dx}$.

(b) Hence, find $\int x\cos(4x) dx$.

### Example

Find $\int (3x+2)^2 dx$.

**Solution**

$$\int (3x+2)^2 dx = \frac{(3x+2)^3}{3} \times \frac{1}{3} + C = \frac{(3x+2)^3}{9} + C.$$

4. Find $\int x(x-2)^2 dx$.

5. Find $\int (5x+7)^{\frac{1}{3}} dx$.

### Example

Find $\int \dfrac{1}{2\sqrt{2x+3}}dx$.

**Solution**

$\int \dfrac{1}{2\sqrt{2x+3}}dx = \sqrt{2x+3} \times \dfrac{1}{4}+C.$

**6** Find $\int \dfrac{1}{\sqrt{x+2}}dx$.

**7** Find $\int (2e^x - 1)^2 dx$.

## 15.2 Definite Integral

### Properties of Definite Integral

Definite integral is considered the net area under the curve $y = f(x)$ from $x = a$ to $x = b$. In fact, we just utilize the indefinite integral to figure out the antiderivative form, then substitute $x = b$ and $x = a$ to find the difference. Hence, the following properties are satisfied.

1. $\int_a^c f(x)dx = \int_a^b f(x)dx + \int_c^b f(x)dx$

2. $\int_a^b f(x)dx = -\int_b^a f(x)dx$

3. $\int_a^a f(x)dx = 0$

**8** Express $\int_1^8 (3\sqrt{x} + \dfrac{2}{\sqrt{x}})dx$ in the form $a + b\sqrt{2}$ where $a$ and $b$ are integers.

**9** Evaluate $\int_0^{\frac{1}{2}} e^{1-2x} dx$.

**10** Solve the following questions.

(a) Differentiate $x^2 \ln(x)$ with respect to $x$.

(b) Hence, show that $\int_1^e 4x\ln(x)dx = e^2 + 1$.

**11** Evaluate
$$\int_0^{\frac{\pi}{6}} \cos(2x+\frac{\pi}{6})dx$$

# Answerkey for Practice Problems

1. $k=3$ and $\int \dfrac{x+5}{\sqrt{2x+15}}dx = \dfrac{x\sqrt{2x+15}}{3}+C.$

2. $\int \dfrac{10}{(3x-1)^4}dx = -\dfrac{10}{9(3x-1)^3}+C.$

3. 

(a) $\sin(4x)+4x\cos(4x)$

(b) $\int x\cos(4x)dx = \dfrac{x}{4}\sin(4x)+\dfrac{1}{16}\cos(4x)+C$

4. $\dfrac{(x-2)^4}{4}+\dfrac{2(x-2)^3}{3}+C.$

5. $\int (5x+7)^{\frac{1}{3}}dx = \dfrac{3}{20}(5x+7)^{\frac{4}{3}}+C$

6. $2(x+2)^{\frac{1}{2}}$

7. $2e^{2x}-4e^{x}+x+C$

8. $-6+40\sqrt{2}$

9. $\dfrac{e-1}{2}$

10. (a) $2x\ln(x)+x$

11. $\dfrac{1}{4}$

# Topic 16

# Bounded Area

✓ Vertical Slicing

✓ Horizontal Slicing

## 16.1 Vertical Slicing

Given $y = f(x)$ bounded by $x = a$ and $x = b$ and $x$-axis, then the area bounded by the curve is equal to

$$\int_a^b f(x)dx$$

where $f(x)dx$ is the area of a rectangle with extremely thin thickness. Given two distinct functions $y = f(x)$ and $y = g(x)$, assume the area is found by vertical slicing. Then the area bounded by the graphs of two functions from $x = a$ to $x = b$ is equal to

$$\int_a^b \text{upper function } - \text{ lower function } dx$$

where upper function can be either $f(x)$ or $g(x)$. One must observe which one is higher than the other.

### Example

Evaluate $\int_2^5 x^2 dx$.

**Solution**

$$\int_2^5 x^2 dx = \frac{5^3}{3} - \frac{2^3}{3} = \frac{125}{3} - \frac{8}{3} = \frac{117}{3} = 39.$$

$\boxed{1}$ Evaluate $\int_3^4 e^{3x} dx$.

2. Evaluate $\int_{\frac{\pi}{6}}^{\frac{\pi}{2}} \sin(x)\,dx$.

3. Find the area bounded by $y = \sin(x)$ and $y = \cos(x)$ from $x = 0$ to $x = \frac{\pi}{4}$.

## 16.2 Horizontal Slicing

Given $x = f(y)$ bounded by $y = c$ and $y = d$ and y-axis, then the area bounded by the curve is equal to

$$\int_c^d f(y)dy$$

where $f(y)dy$ is the area of a rectangle with extremely thin thickness. Given two distinct curves $x = f(y)$ and $x = g(y)$, assume the area is found by horizontal slicing. Then the area bounded by the two curves from $y = c$ to $y = d$ is equal to

$$\int_c^d \text{right function} - \text{left function } dx$$

where right function can be either $x = f(y)$ or $x = g(y)$. One must observe which one is placed right of the other. Sometimes $x = f(y)$ is not explicitly given. In such case, one must find the inverse function.

### Example

Evaluate the area of region bounded by $y = 2$, $y = 3$, $y = \ln(x)$, and the y-axis.

**Solution**

In order to apply horizontal slicing, we turn $y = \ln(x)$ into $x = e^y$. Apply horizontal slicing. The area of the region is $\int_2^3 e^y dy = e^3 - e^2$.

---

**4** Calculate the area of region bounded by $x = (y-3)^2$ and $x = 1$.

**5** Calculate the area of region bounded by $y = \ln(x)$ from $y = 0$ to $y = 2$.

**6** Calculate the area of region bounded by $x = y^2$, $y = -1$, $y = 3$ and $x = 0$.

## Answerkey for Practice Problems

1. $\dfrac{e^{12} - e^9}{3}$

2. $\dfrac{\sqrt{3}}{2}$

3. $\sqrt{2} - 1$

4. $\dfrac{4}{3}$

5. $e^2 - 1$

6. $\dfrac{28}{3}$

# Topic 17

# Kinematics

✓ Motion on a Straight Line

## 17.1 Motion on a Straight Line

If an object $P$ moves along a straight line, then $s(t)$ is a displacement function for time $t$. This measures the displacement from the origin $O$. Hence, $s(0)$ is the initial position of $P$ at $t = 0$.

1. $s(t) > 0$ : $P$ is located at the right of $O$ at time $t$.

2. $s(t) = 0$ : $P$ is located at the right of $O$ at time $t$.

3. $s(t) < 0$ : $P$ is located at the left of $O$ at time $t$.

Assume there is a displacement function for a particle on a line $L$, given by $s = f(t)$. Then the velocity and acceleration function is given by

$$v(t) = \frac{ds}{dt} \iff \int v(t)dt = s(t) + C$$

$$a(t) = \frac{dv}{dt} = \frac{d^2s}{dt^2} \iff \int a(t)dt = v(t) + C$$

In other words, we can take the integration to figure out $s(t)$ from $v(t)$ and $v(t)$ from $a(t)$. When we integrate $v(t)$ to find out displacement, we are not getting the total distance travelled by the particle because there might be some parts that are cancelled out as the particle moves back and forth. Therefore, we need to distinguish the two concepts carefully.

1. Displacement : $\int v(t)dt$

2. Distance traveled : $\int |v(t)|dt$

For instance, the distance traveled by the particle in the following figure is 5, but the displacement of the particle is 1.

As one can see from the real number line above,

$$\int v(t)dt \leq \int |v(t)|dt$$

**1** A particle moves in a straight line so that $t$ seconds after passing a fixed point $O$ its acceleration $a$ m/s$^2$ is given by $a = 6t - 12$. Given that its speed at $O$ is 16m/s, find

(a) the values of $t$ at which the particle is stationary.

(b) the total distance the particle travels in the fifth second.

**2** A particle travels in a straight line so that $t$ seconds after passing through a fixed point $O$, its displacement $s$ m from $O$ is given by $s = \ln(t^2 + 2)$.

(a) Find the value of $t$ when $s = 3$.

(b) Find the distance traveled by the particle during the two second.

(c) Find the acceleration of the particle when $t = 3$.

3. A particle moves in a straight line so that, $t$ seconds after leaving a fixed point $O$, its velocity $v$ is given by $v = 3e^{2t} + 3t$.

(a) Find the initial velocity of the particle.

(b) Find the initial acceleration of the particle.

(c) Find the total distance travelled by the particle in the two second.

**4** A particle travels in a straight line so that $t$ seconds after passing through a fixed point $O$, its velocity, $v$ m/s is given by $v = 6\sin(\frac{t}{2})$. Find the distance if the particle from $O$ when it first comes to instantaneous rest.

# Answerkey for Practice Problems

**1.**

(a) $v(t)$ is always greater than 0. There is no value of $t$ when the particle is stationary.

(b) 55

**2.**

(a) $\sqrt{e^3 - 2}$

(b) $\ln(3)$

(c) $-\dfrac{14}{121}$

**3.**

(a) 3

(b) 9

(c) $\dfrac{3e^4 + 9}{2}$

**4.** The total distance traveled is 24.

# Topic 18

# Vectors

- ✓ Geometric Vectors
- ✓ Coordinate Vectors
- ✓ Vector Algebra

## 18.1 Geometric Vectors

Vector, denoted by $\vec{v}$ or **v**, is defined as a quantity that has both a magnitude and a direction. It is usually represented by an arrow in the plane or in space. The length of the arrow is its magnitude and the direction of the arrow is its direction.

Two arrows with the same magnitude and direction represent the same vector.

The starting point of the vector is called the tail and the end as the tip or head. Also, the vector between two points $X$ and $Y$ is denoted $\overrightarrow{XY}$.

Here, $X$ is called the initial point and $Y$ the terminal point of $\overrightarrow{XY}$. The magnitude of the vector $\vec{v}$ is denoted $\|\vec{v}\|$. Magnitude is either called length or norm, which is computed by the usual distance formula.

Scaling a vector means changing its length by a scale factor. In fact, this is simply multiplying or dividing vector quantity by a number. Two non-zero vectors are parallel if a vector is a scalar multiple of the other.

### Parallel Vectors

$\vec{a} = k\vec{b}$ for some constant $k$.

Furthermore, if a vector is scaled down by its own length, such vector is called a unit vector, $\hat{v} = \dfrac{\vec{v}}{|v|}$

## 18.2 Coordinate Vectors

The method of representing a vector in a coordinate plane requires two setups.

1. Tail of the vector at the Origin $(0,0)$

2. Head of the vectors at $(a,b)$

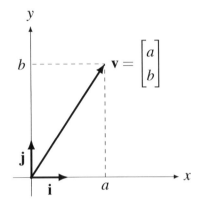

The Cartesian coordinate can be used to represent vectors with the given origin. If the head coordinates are $(x,y)$, then we have two associated vectors.

1. $\begin{bmatrix} x \\ y \end{bmatrix}$ is a column vector.

2. $\begin{bmatrix} x & y \end{bmatrix}$ is a row vector.

A column vector is useful when a vector is expressed as a linear combination of $\mathbf{i},\mathbf{j}$. For instance,

$$\begin{bmatrix} 3 \\ 4 \end{bmatrix} = 3\begin{bmatrix} 1 \\ 0 \end{bmatrix} + 4\begin{bmatrix} 0 \\ 1 \end{bmatrix} = \begin{bmatrix} 1 & 0 \\ 0 & 1 \end{bmatrix}\begin{bmatrix} 3 \\ 4 \end{bmatrix}$$

The usefulness of this representation will be covered in an IB coursework.

**1** Find the length of the vector $\begin{bmatrix} 2 \\ 3 \end{bmatrix}$.

## 18.3 Vector Algebra

Recall that a position vector is a vector that originates from the origin $O$. Then, we can deduce the vectors connecting the three points $O, A, B$ as

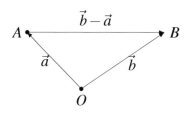

Notice that we do not break away from the usual vector algebra of parallelogram law or triangle law. In fact, $\vec{a} + (\vec{b} - \vec{a}) = \vec{b}$.

### Golden Rule

$$\overrightarrow{OA} + \overrightarrow{AB} = \overrightarrow{OB} \qquad\qquad \overrightarrow{OB} - \overrightarrow{OA} = \overrightarrow{AB}$$

**2** In the following diagram, the position vectors of points $A$ and $B$ relative to $O$ are $\vec{a}$ and $\vec{b}$ respectively. Assume that the lines $AB$ and $OP$ intersect at $Q$. Given that $\overrightarrow{BP} = 2(\vec{a} + \vec{b})$ and $\overrightarrow{AQ} = \lambda \overrightarrow{AB}$ and $\overrightarrow{OQ} = \mu \overrightarrow{OP}$, express $\overrightarrow{OQ}$ in terms of

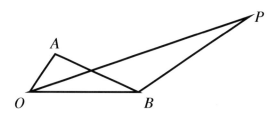

(a) $\lambda, \vec{a}, \vec{b}$ \qquad (b) $\mu, \vec{a}, \vec{b}$ \qquad (c) hence, evaluate $\lambda$ and $\mu$.

**3** Given that $\overrightarrow{OA} = \vec{a}$, $\overrightarrow{OC} = \vec{b}$, and $\overrightarrow{OC} = 3\overrightarrow{OB}$, express $\overrightarrow{AB}$ and $\overrightarrow{AC}$ in terms of $\vec{a}$ and $\vec{b}$. Given that $\overrightarrow{AX} = 2\overrightarrow{XB}$ and $\overrightarrow{AY} = k\overrightarrow{YC}$, express $\overrightarrow{OX}$ and $\overrightarrow{OY}$ in terms of $\vec{a}, \vec{b}$ and $k$. If the points $O, X$ and $Y$ lie in a straight line, find $k$.

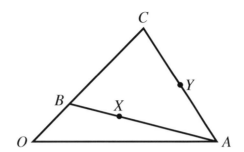

When a vector question comes out in your test, either for midterms, finals, or IGCSE tests, you have two options to solve this type of questions. You can simply use Algebra, i.e., $\overrightarrow{XY} = \overrightarrow{OY} - \overrightarrow{OX}$ or $\overrightarrow{OX} + \overrightarrow{XY} = \overrightarrow{OY}$. Or, you can use vector geometry to solve it with better visualization.

**4** If $\overrightarrow{OA} = \mathbf{p} + \mathbf{q}$ and $\overrightarrow{OB} = 2\mathbf{p} - \mathbf{q}$, where **p** and **q** are two vectors and M is the midpoint of AB. Find in terms of **p** and **q**,

(a) $\overrightarrow{AB}$

(b) $\overrightarrow{AM}$

(c) $\overrightarrow{OM}$

5. The position vectors of A and B are **a** and **b**, respectively, relative to an origin $O$. $C$ is the midpoint of $AB$, and $D$ divides $OB$ in the ratio of $2:1$. $AD$ and $OC$ meet at $P$.

(a) Taking $\overrightarrow{OP} = p\overrightarrow{OC}$ and $\overrightarrow{AP} = q\overrightarrow{AD}$, express $\overrightarrow{OP}$ in two different forms.

(b) Find the values of $p$ and $q$.

(c) Find the ratio of $\overrightarrow{OP} : \overrightarrow{PC}$.

# Answerkey for Practice Problems

1. $\sqrt{13}$

02.

(a) $(1-\lambda)\vec{a}+\lambda\vec{b}$

(b) $2\mu\vec{a}+3\mu\vec{b}$

(c) $\mu=\dfrac{1}{5}, \lambda=\dfrac{3}{5}$

03. $\overrightarrow{AB}=\dfrac{1}{3}\vec{b}-\vec{a}$, $\overrightarrow{AC}=\vec{b}-\vec{a}$, $\overrightarrow{OX}=\dfrac{1}{3}\vec{a}+\dfrac{2}{9}\vec{b}$, $\overrightarrow{OY}=\dfrac{1}{k+1}\vec{a}+\dfrac{k}{k+1}\vec{b}$, and $k=\dfrac{2}{3}$

04.

(a) $\mathbf{p}-2\mathbf{q}$

(b) $\dfrac{1}{2}\mathbf{p}-\mathbf{q}$

(c) $\dfrac{3}{2}\mathbf{p}$

05.

(a) $\dfrac{p}{2}\mathbf{a}+\dfrac{p}{2}\mathbf{b}$, $(1-q)\mathbf{a}+\dfrac{2q}{3}\mathbf{b}$

(b) $p=\dfrac{4}{5}, q=\dfrac{3}{5}$

(c) $4:1$

# Topic 19

# Relative Velocity

✓ True Velocity and Relative Velocity

✓ Relative Motion in a Current or Air

✓ Relative Motion of Two Moving Objects

## 19.1 True Velocity and Relative Velocity

First, true velocity of an object is the velocity relative to the earth, known as a true(or actual) velocity. The true speed $V_A$ is also known as the ground speed.

On the other hand, a relative velocity requires two moving objects. For instance, if $A$ moves 2m/s east and $B$ moves 1m/s east, and $B$ stays further east from $A$, then $B$ would feel $A$ approaching him with the speed of 1m/s. This is known as $V_{A/B}$, read as the velocity of $A$ relative to $B$. The following equation shows the famous relative velocity equation.

$$V_{B/A} + V_A = V_B$$

The best way to remember this relative velocity concept is to visualize when you drive. The cars on the opposite lane seem to drive faster than you think because they drive the opposite direction from you. However, the cars on your lane seem to drive slowly because their directions are not different from yours.

**1** In an airport, a straight horizontal moving walkway is designed to travel at 0.8m/s in a direction from a fixed point $A$ to another fixed point $B$. A passenger $P$ walks from $A$ to $B$ on the walkway, at a speed of 1.2m/s relative to the walkway. At the same instant, another passenger $Q$ walks from $A$ to $B$, on a fixed horizontal ground alongside the walkway at a speed of 1.5m/s. Calculate the velocity of $P$ and the speed of $P$ relative to $Q$.

## 19.2 Relative Motion in a Current or Air

There are two types of relative motion in a current: motion in water and in air. Typically, the questions lay out multiple sets of information. One thing to remember is that the actual velocity is not usually given to us, but the relative velocity is given to us. Look out for phrases "in still air" or "in still water." It means that the velocity of a boat, a plane or a swimmer relative to water or air being fixed is provided in a numerical value. First, let's look at an example of motion in water. In any case of a relative motion question, we use $V_{B/A} + V_A = V_B$.

$\boxed{2}$ If a river is flowing at 4m/s due east and a boat, of speed 3m/s in still water, is steered in the direction due north, find the true speed and direction of motion of the boat.

For an object $P$ moving in the water, the course taken by $P$ in the direction of $V_{P/W}$, the velocity of $P$ relative to $W$, the water.

**3** A boy swims at 1m/s in still water is crossing a river 20m wide. The river flows between parallel banks at 1.5m/s. He heads upstream in a direction making an angle of 60° with the bank. Find

(a) the speed at which he travels.

(b) the angle which his resultant velocity makes with the bank

(c) the time taken for the crossing.

For an object $P$ flying in the air, the speed of $P$ in still air is $V_{P/W}$ and the course taken by $P$ is the direction of $V_{P/W}$ where $V_{P/W}$ is the velocity of $P$ relative to the wind $W$.

**4** The speed of an aircraft in still air is 600km/h. The wind velocity is 160km/h from the west. The aircraft is steered on the course in the direction $060°$. Find the true velocity of the aircraft.

## 19.3 Relative Motion of Two Moving Objects

For two moving objects with $V_P$ and $V_Q$, true velocities, then we have

$$V_Q = V_{Q/P} + V_P$$
$$V_P = V_{P/Q} + V_Q$$

First, there is a relative path question, which requires us to draw vectors to solve the questions. When drawing vectors, make sure you put the terminal points together to figure out the relative velocity.

**5** Two ships $A$ and $B$ are 10 miles apart and move with constant speeds and directions such that $A$ moves with the bearing of $060°$ and the velocity of 10km/h and $B$ moves with the bearing of $330°$ and the velocity of 8km/h. Find the speed and direction of $A$ relative to $B$. Hence, find the distance between $A$ and $B$ when $A$ is due south of $B$.

Second, there is an intercept question, which makes an object $B$ to intercept $A$ or vice versa. Intercept question is not different from a relative path question except that we need to orient a vector to make a horizontal vector for relative velocity. If this sentence is too difficult to comprehend, let's look at the following example.

**6** Two riders $A$ and $B$ are 120m apart with $B$ due east of $A$. Rider $A$ travels 3m/s in a direction of $030°$ and a rider $B$ travels 3.8m/s in a direction $X$. Find the value of $X$ such that a rider $B$ intercepts $A$.

**7** Two riders $A$ and $B$ are 120m apart with $B$ due east of $A$. Rider $A$ travels 4m/s in a direction of $030°$ and a rider $B$ travels 3.8m/s in a direction $X$. Find the value of $X$ such that a rider $B$ intercepts $A$.

# Answerkey for Practice Problems

1. 0.5m/s

2. 053.1301° in bearing; 36.8699° from the bank.

3.

(a) 1.3288

(b) 40.8934°

(c) 9.89743 seconds

4. 468.319km/h

5. The speed is $\sqrt{164}$mph, and the direction is 098.7° in bearing. The distance between $A$ and $B$ is 1.53 miles.

6. The value of $X$ is 313.134° in bearing.

7. The value of $X$ is 335.728° in bearing.

Made in the USA
Las Vegas, NV
13 January 2021